T0113076

21-DAY VEGAN RAW FOOD DIET PLAN

21-DAY VEGAN RAW FOOD DIET PLAN

75 Satisfying Recipes to Revitalize Your Body

HEATHER BOWEN

Photography by Darren Muir

ROCKRIDGE PRESS

Copyright © 2020 by Rockridge Press, Emeryville, California

No part of this publication may be reproduced, stored in a retrieval system, or transmitted in any form or by any means, electronic, mechanical, photocopying, recording, scanning, or otherwise, except as permitted under Sections 107 or 108 of the 1976 United States Copyright Act, without the prior written permission of the Publisher. Requests to the Publisher for permission should be addressed to the Permissions Department, Rockridge Press, 6005 Shellmound Street, Suite 175, Emeryville, CA 94608.

Limit of Liability/Disclaimer of Warranty: The Publisher and the author make no representations or warranties with respect to the accuracy or completeness of the contents of this work and specifically disclaim all warranties, including without limitation warranties of fitness for a particular purpose. No warranty may be created or extended by sales or promotional materials. The advice and strategies contained herein may not be suitable for every situation. This work is sold with the understanding that the Publisher is not engaged in rendering medical, legal, or other professional advice or services. If professional assistance is required, the services of a competent professional person should be sought. Neither the Publisher nor the author shall be liable for damages arising herefrom. The fact that an individual, organization, or website is referred to in this work as a citation and/or potential source of further information does not mean that the author or the Publisher endorses the information the individual, organization, or website may provide or recommendations they/it may make. Further, readers should be aware that websites listed in this work may have changed or disappeared between when this work was written and when it is read.

For general information on our other products and services or to obtain technical support, please contact our Customer Care Department within the United States at (866) 744-2665, or outside the United States at (510) 253-0500.

Rockridge Press publishes its books in a variety of electronic and print formats. Some content that appears in print may not be available in electronic books, and vice versa.

TRADEMARKS: Rockridge Press and the Rockridge Press logo are trademarks or registered trademarks of Callisto Media Inc. and/or its affiliates, in the United States and other countries, and may not be used without written permission. All other trademarks are the property of their respective owners. Rockridge Press is not associated with any product or vendor mentioned in this book.

Interior and Cover Designer: Amanda Kirk

Art Producer: Janice Ackerman

Editor: Daniel Edward Petrino

Production Editor: Mia Moran

Photography © 2020 Darren Muir. Food styling by Yolanda Muir

Author photo © 2020 Iain Mains

ISBN: Print 978-1-64611-719-2 | eBook 978-1-64611-720-8

R0

THIS BOOK IS DEDICATED TO
my friends and family.
Without your love and support,
I would not be where I am today.
I am forever grateful for you all.

Contents

INTRODUCTION

I was introduced to raw food in college, when a family friend made a raw food dessert from nuts and dates. I was enthralled! I decided I needed to know more about this way of eating. Exploring my friend's pantry and kitchen, I found it full of nuts, seeds, legumes, dried fruit, and fresh produce. I was amazed at the variety of dishes that could be created with such simple, healthy ingredients. My passion for food and nutrition was ignited, and off I went to Vancouver, British Columbia, to pursue my dream of becoming a nutritionist. Four years later, with a BSc degree in hand, I found myself inspired to take my passion for nutrition even further, so I continued studying holistic nutrition and became a raw food chef.

I witnessed a powerful transformation in myself when I eliminated convenient, processed, and packaged foods and replaced them with wholesome plant-based foods. My skin cleared up, my debilitating irritable bowel symptoms went away, and my brain fog dissipated. My hormones balanced themselves out, I was less emotional and reactive, my energy skyrocketed, and I lost 15 pounds of excess weight. I was a new woman! Armed with my blender, food processor, and dehydrator, I was on a quest to change the world, one plant-based recipe at a time.

Most people who know they need to improve their health and "eat better" really don't know where to start and are easily overwhelmed and confused by all the conflicting information out there. Some vegan diets consist mainly of processed and convenient simple carbohydrates such as potato chips and pasta. Although they are not consuming animal products, their diet is devoid of fiber, protein, and fat, which can wreak havoc on the insulin-secreting pancreas and may lead to type 2 diabetes.

My goal in writing this book is to provide you with the tools and empower you with the knowledge to become your own nutritional healer. I have created a 21-day vegan raw food meal plan that will ensure all your nutritional needs are met, calories are sufficient, and taste buds satisfied. I have taken all the guesswork out for you so all you have to do is follow my instructions, recipes, and meal plan, and I assure you, you will feel amazing. I encourage you to stick it out for the entire 21 days, as that is how long it takes to develop a habit—and what a habit to develop! Even if your diet after the 21 days stays at just 75 percent unprocessed, whole plant-based foods, that is still better than nothing, and you should be darn proud of yourself! You will not only save yourself time by following a plan, but you will also save yourself money by purchasing legumes over animal products—and staying away from the doctor's office.

Good luck! You've got this!

1

WELCOME TO THE VEGAN RAW FOOD DIET

Welcome to the world of raw and living foods! Are you ready for a total body revolution? This vegan raw food cookbook and 21-day meal plan will reboot your entire system. It's a transformative experience that will reset your biology and metabolism, enabling you to reverse chronic symptoms and effortlessly break free of your cravings. Just by changing your diet, you can quickly and profoundly change your life. The goal of this chapter is to introduce you to the world of raw food and veganism, elaborating on the nutrition and health benefits of this diet. Common questions will be answered, assuring you that this lifestyle is a lot easier than you may think.

A BRIEF INTRODUCTION TO THE RAW VEGAN DIET

A raw vegan diet combines the principles of veganism and raw foodism. Like veganism, it excludes all foods of animal origin, but it also includes raw foodism practice, where food is eaten in its natural state, completely raw or heated at temperatures below 118°F. When food is heated above that temperature, vital nutrients and enzymes are destroyed. Alternative meal preparation methods, such as juicing, blending, soaking, sprouting, and dehydrating, are used instead of cooking. A raw vegan diet is rich in unprocessed, whole plant foods such as fruits, fatty fruits like avocado and coconut, berries, vegetables, nuts, seeds, and sprouted grains and legumes. In addition, there are no recipes in this book containing animal products or cooked grains, which naturally minimizes many foods likely to cause allergies.

As with all new diets, it's important to consult with your physician before making any drastic changes to what you eat; please make this a first step in embarking on this adventure.

The raw food diet is not about deprivation; in fact, you can still enjoy all the comfort foods. It's a chance to shift your perspective and discover an entire new world of fresh foods prepared in ways that maintain integrity and freshness.

COMMON QUESTIONS

Eating raw is not a new idea. In fact, it may well be the oldest way of eating known to humankind. Although cooking food is now common practice around the world, raw vegan diets are the latest rage, with raw vegan restaurants, recipe books, and blogs popping up all around us. As the saying goes, what's old is new again, and nowadays, raw is hot and vegan is hotter.

Although raw diets may be old as humankind, there are doubts about their nutritional viability and concerns about the time and effort required to prepare. We have taken the most common questions and concerns that people have when embarking on a raw vegan diet and answered them here.

What can I eat on the vegan raw food diet?

The road to raw veganism is not one of limitation or restriction. In this book, we have included all your favorite comfort foods: pizza, bread, muffins, cookies, crackers, and pasta. The only difference is that these products are prepared with whole, sprouted grains and legumes, soaked nuts and seeds, and fresh fruits and vegetables. Because these foods are prepared below a temperature of 118°F, they still contain the enzymes necessary to properly digest and assimilate nutrients. Any foods that have the words roasted, dry-roasted, toasted, cooked, or baked on the label are not raw. Neither are canned foods.

Can I use frozen foods?

Frozen fruits are definitely acceptable on the vegan raw food diet. In fact, frozen fruit is sometimes more nutrient dense than fresh fruit that may have lost its nutritional value due to being over- or underripe and then held in atmosphere-controlled environments for travel purposes. Frozen fruit, on the other hand, is picked at the perfect ripeness and flash frozen immediately to maintain its freshness. Frozen fruit is also a convenient way to keep a variety of fruits and berries on hand that can easily be thrown into a smoothie or infused water. Frozen vegetables, however, are not accepted on the raw food diet. See the "Freeze It" section in chapter 2 (page 21) for more information on freezing.

Where will I get my protein?

Plants! There are 20 amino acids that combine to make a complete protein. Of these, 12 are essential and need to be obtained from food because the body cannot make them. By consuming a variety of plant-based proteins, such as nuts and seeds, sprouted grains and legumes, green algae like chlorella and spirulina, edamame beans, soy beans, and hemp seeds, in addition to fruits and vegetables, your body will get all the amino acids it needs to build complete proteins.

Is tofu acceptable on a raw diet?

Tofu is made by processing soybeans using high heat. Therefore, stick to raw edamame beans as your soy-based protein. They are a great addition to smoothies, salads, blended soups, or eaten as a snack, and they are a great source of protein and omega-3 fatty acids. Make sure to look for that non-GMO label on the package, as soy products are often highly genetically modified. (Also note that any product with the USDA "Certified Organic" label is by definition non-GMO.)

Can I heat my food at all?

Yes, you can use a dehydrator set at no more than 118°F. The temperature of the food cannot go above 118°F or the living enzymes will be destroyed and your food will no longer be considered raw. You can also use warm water in your blended soups to enjoy a warm soup on a cold day. Drinking warm water is actually encouraged, as it takes a lot of energy for your body to warm up the water for proper digestion.

What benefits can I expect?

Health benefits are endless on a raw vegan diet. You are encouraged to follow the 21-day meal plan to ensure sufficient nutrients and calories and to see the full effect of its healing benefits. Depending on your starting point, the health benefits will vary; however, most people report an improved sense of energy and vitality, better digestion, clearer skin, and weight loss. There have also been cases where chronic health conditions such as type 2 diabetes, cardiovascular disease, and even some cancers have been reversed.

Will I lose weight?

People eating raw foods find that it's easier to achieve their optimal weight. When you receive true nourishment, food cravings and addictions tend to disappear. Your hunger is satisfied because the body has the essential nutrients it needs. The healthy fats you will consume in the nuts, seeds, and fatty fruits will signal the appetite hormone leptin to tell your brain you are satisfied. The fats and fiber in this plan will balance your blood sugar so the fat storage hormone insulin will not be stimulated. Following a meal plan will also keep you accountable and prevent overeating throughout the day.

How will I know I am getting all my nutrients and enough calories?

The 21-day meal plan is specifically created to make sure all your macronutrients and micronutrients are met. The raw vegan diet doesn't consist solely of fruit and vegetables. In addition to the essential antioxidants and fiber found in produce, you will also be consuming high-fat nuts and seeds and fatty fruits such as coconut and avocado. These will keep you feeling satisfied. In fact, each meal is carefully designed to ensure a proper balance of fibrous carbohydrates, healthy fats, and satisfying clean protein.

NUTRITION ON THE VEGAN RAW FOOD DIET

The main importance of eating whole plant foods in their natural state without processing or cooking is to ensure that the enzymes remain intact and are not denatured in the heating process. The live enzymes in raw foods are necessary for digestion and absorption of nutrients. This reduces the dependency on the body to produce the necessary enzymes, which eventually deplete, causing inflammation and allergies.

While some people follow the vegan raw food diet for ethical or environmental reasons, most choose to follow it for its health benefits. Weight loss, improved heart health, better digestion, and lowered risk of diabetes and cancer are some of the reasons people find the vegan raw food diet life changing. They are amazed that something so simple could make such a profound difference in their health, mood, and energy. When you eat a diet of raw, whole plant-based foods, food becomes your medicine, gradually healing the body by providing essential nutrients. Most people experience some difference within the first few days and deeper healing after 21 days.

This book is a catalyst for change, a cutting-edge plan that steers clear of inflammatory choices such as white sugar, harmful fats, and processed foods and replaces them with healthy choices such as natural unrefined sweeteners, healing fats, and anti-inflammatory vegetables.

A fully raw vegan diet may pose some health risks if not properly planned or executed. Following our 21-day meal plan of nutritionally designed and balanced recipes, you will get the sufficient amount of calories, properly balanced macronutrients, and the recommended daily allowance of micronutrients. If you have any serious health conditions or are pregnant, please consult your health-care provider before embarking on this raw vegan journey.

Below is a nutritional information table that highlights the calories and key nutrients per serving of many of the ingredients included in the 21-day meal plan. This is a great guide for calculating calories and nutrients for each meal. Fiber is the best nutrient for gut health and at least 30 grams should be consumed per day. Protein is the nutrient most in question on a vegan diet and the suggested RDA is 0.8 grams per kilogram of body weight, or 0.36 grams per pound.

Fruit, Vegetables, Nuts, Seeds & Legumes Nutritional Information

ITEM	SERVING SIZE	CALORIES PER SERVING	KEY NUTRIENTS PER SERVING		
			FIBER	PROTEIN	MICRONUTRIENTS
FRUITS					
Apples	1 medium, 180 g	80	4.4 g	0.5 g	Vitamin C: 8.4 mg
Avocado	1 cup diced, 150 g	240	10.0 g	3.0 g	Vitamin E: 3.1 mg; Vitamin K: 31.5 mcg
Bananas	1 medium, 130 g	105	3.1 g	1.2 g	Potassium: 422.4 mg; Vitamin B6: 0.4 mg
Blueberries	1 cup, 148 g	84	3.6 g	1.1 g	Vitamin K: 28.6 mcg; Vitamin C: 14.4 mg

ITEM	SERVING SIZE	CALORIES PER SERVING	KEY NUTRIENTS PER SERVING		
			FIBER	PROTEIN	MICRONUTRIENTS
Figs, dried	3	120	10.5 g	0.4 g	Vitamin B6: 0.2 mg
Grapefruit	1 medium, 128 g	80	2.8 g	0.8 g	Vitamin C: 88.1 mg; Vitamin A: 118.7 mcg RAE (Retinol Activity Equivalents); Potassium: 355.8 mg
Grapes	1 cup, 151 g	104	1.4 g	1.1 g	Vitamin K: 22.1 mcg; Copper: 0.2 mg; Vitamin B2: 0.1 mg
Lemon, Lime, juice	¼ cup, 61 g	13	0.9 g	0.2 g	Vitamin C: 23.6 mg; Folate: 12.2 mcg
Orange	1 medium, 131 g	62	3.1 g	1.2 g	Vitamin C: 69.7 mg; Folate: 39.3 mcg; Calcium: 52.4 mg
Pear	1 medium, 178 g	100	5.5 g	0.6 g	Copper: 0.2 mg; Vitamin C: 7.7 mg
Pineapple	1 cup, 165 g	83	2.3 g	0.9 g	Vitamin C: 78.9 mg; Manganese: 1.5 mg; Copper: 0.2 mg
Raspberries	1 cup, 123 g	64	8.0 g	1.5 g	Vitamin C: 32.2 mg; Manganese: 0.8 mg
Strawberries	1 cup, 144 g	45	2.9 g	1.0 g	Vitamin C: 84.7 mg; Folate: 34.6 mcg; Iodine: 13.0 mcg
Watermelon	1 cup, 152 g	46	0.6 g	0.9 g	Vitamin C: 12.3 mg; Vitamin A: 43.2 mcg RAE
VEGETABLES					
Alfalfa sprouts	1 cup, 33 g	8	0.6 g	1.3 g	Vitamin K: 10.1 mcg; Folate: 11.9 mcg; Potassium: 26.1 mg
Asparagus	1 cup, 180 g	40	3.6 g	4.2 g	Vitamin K: 91.1 mcg; Folate: 268.2 mcg; Copper: 0.3 mg
Beets	1 cup, 170 g	75	3.4 g	2.9 g	Folate: 136.0 mcg; Manganese: 0.6 mg; Copper: 0.1 mg
Bell pepper, red	1 cup, 92 g	29	1.9 g	0.9 g	Vitamin C: 117.5 mg; Vitamin A: 144.0 mcg RAE; Vitamin B6: 0.3 mg

ITEM	SERVING SIZE	CALORIES PER SERVING	KEY NUTRIENTS PER SERVING		
			FIBER	PROTEIN	MICRONUTRIENTS
Bok choy	1 cup, 170 g	20	1.7 g	2.7 g	Vitamin K: 57.8 mcg; Vitamin C: 44.2 mg; Vitamin A: 361.2 mcg RAE; Folate: 69.7 mcg; Calcium: 62.4 mg; Potassium: 630.7 mg
Broccoli	1 cup, 156 g	55	5.2 g	3.7 g	Vitamin K: 220.1 mcg; Vitamin C: 101.2 mg; Folate: 168.5 mcg; Calcium: 62.4 mg,
Cabbage	1 cup, 89g	22	2.2 g	1.1 g	Vitamin C: 32.6 mg; Vitamin K: 67.6 mcg; Folate: 38.3 mcg
Carrots	1 cup sliced, 122 g	50	3.4 g	1.1 g	Vitamin A: 1019.1 mcg RAE; Biotin: 6.1 mcg; Vitamin B6: 0.2 mg
Cauliflower	1 cup, 124 g	29	2.7 g	2.3 g	Vitamin C: 54.9 mg; Vitamin K: 17.1 mcg; Folate: 54.6 mcg; Vitamin B6: 0.2 mg
Celery	1 cup, 101 g	16	1.4 g	0.7 g	Vitamin K: 29.6 mcg; Folate: 36.4 mcg; Potassium: 262.6 mg
Cilantro	½ cup, 8 g	2	0.2 g	0.2 g	Vitamin K: 24.8 mcg; Vitamin A: 27.0 mcg RAE; Vitamin C: 2.2 mg
Cucumber	1 cup, 104 g	16	0.5 g	0.7 g	Vitamin K: 17.1 mcg; Molybdenum 5.2 mcg; Pantothenic acid: 0.3 mg
Kale	1 cup, 16 g	8	0.6 g	0.7 g	Calcium: 24.0 mg; Iron: 0.2 mg; Potassium: 79.0 mg
Romaine lettuce	2 cups, 94 g	16	2.0 g	1.2 g	Vitamin K: 96.4 mcg; Vitamin A: 409.4 mcg RAE; Folate: 127.8 mcg
Parsley	½ cup, chopped	11	1.0 g	0.9 g	Vitamin K: 498.6 mcg; Vitamin C: 40.4 mg; Vitamin A: 128.0 mcg RAE
Spinach	1 cup, 30 g	7	0.7 g	0.9 g	Calcium: 30.0 mg; Iron: 0.8 mg; Potassium: 167.0 mg
Sea vegetables, dulse, dried	1 T, 5 g	11	0.1 g	1.8 g	Iodine: 750.0 mcg; Vitamin C: 12.2 mg; Vitamin B2: 0.1 mg
Zucchini	1 cup, chopped (124 g)	20	1.4g	1.5g	Vitamin C: 21.1 mg; Riboflavin: 0.2 mg; Vitamin B6: 0.3 mg

ITEM	SERVING SIZE	CALORIES PER SERVING	KEY NUTRIENTS PER SERVING		
			FIBER	PROTEIN	MICRONUTRIENTS
NUTS					
Almonds	¼ cup, 23 g	132	2.8 g	4.9 g	Biotin: 14.7 mcg; Vitamin E: 6.0 mg (ATE); Copper: 0.2 mg
Brazil nuts	¼ cup, 28 g	186	2.1 g	4.1 g	Selenium: 828.8 mcg; Calcium: 53.3 mg; Magnesium: 125 mg
Cashews	¼ cup, 40 g	221	1.3 g	7.3 g	Copper: 0.9 mg; Phosphorus: 237.2 mg; Magnesium: 116.8 mg
Coconut	¼ cup	100	2.0 g	1.0 g	Sodium: 5.0 mg
Hazelnuts	¼ cup, 28 g	212	3.3 g	5 g	Vitamin E: 6.7 mg; Manganese: 1.8 mg; Copper: 0.5 mg
Pecans	¼ cup, 28 g	188	2.6 g	2.5 g	Manganese: 1.2 mg; Omega-3: 268.8 mg
Pine nuts	¼ cup, 28 g	191	1.0 g	3.9 g	Vitamin E: 3.2 mcg; Vitamin K: 18.2 mcg; Manganese: 3.0 mg
Walnuts	¼ cup, 30 g	196	2.0g	4.6 g	Omega-3: 2.7 g; Copper: 0.5 mg; Manganese: 1.0 mg
SEEDS					
Chia seeds	¼ cup, 46 g	240	16.0 g	8.0 g	Omega-3: 8.0 g; Calcium: 290.8 mg; Magnesium: 167.5 mg
Flaxseed, ground	¼ cup, 28 g	150	7.6 g	5.2 g	Omega-3: 6.4 g; Vitamin B1: 0.4 mg; Copper 0.4 mg
Hemp seeds	¼ cup, 40 g	240	1.4 g	13.4 g	Boron, Omega-3: 3.4 g; Calcium: 26.6 mg; Potassium: 466.6 mg
Pumpkin seeds	¼ cup, 32 g	180	2.0 g	9.8 g	Manganese: 1.4 mg; Phosphorus: 400.0 mg; Copper: 0.4 mg
Sesame seeds	¼ cup, 36 g	206	4.2 g	6.4 g	Copper: 1.4 mg; Manganese: 1.0 mg; Calcium: 352.0 mg
Sunflower seeds	¼ cup, 40 g	204	3.0 g	7.2 g	Vitamin E: 12.4 mg (ATE); Copper: 0.6 mg; Vitamin B1: 0.6 mg
Quinoa	¼ cup dry, sprouted, 44 g	170	4.0 g	5.0 g	Folate: 77.7 mcg, Magnesium: 83.7 mg; Iron: 1.94 mg

ITEM	SERVING SIZE	CALORIES PER SERVING	KEY NUTRIENTS PER SERVING		
			FIBER	PROTEIN	MICRONUTRIENTS
LEGUMES					
Chickpeas	¼ cup dry, 50 g	189	6.0 g	10.0 g	Calcium: 20.1 g; Iron: 1.2 mg
Lentils	¼ cup dry, sprouted, 39 g	150	10.0 g	9.0 g	Iron: 3.0 mg; Calcium: 26 mg; Potassium: 264 mg

Sources: Krause's Food, Nutrition, & Diet Therapy, 11th Edition, by L. Kathleen Mahan and Sylvia Escott-Stump.

The World's Healthiest Foods. www.whfoods.org.

SUPPLEMENTS ON A VEGAN RAW FOOD DIET

To meet the recommended daily allowances (RDA) of micronutrients on the vegan raw food diet, a few supplements are helpful because certain micronutrients are more prevalent and bioavailable in animal sources. Some of the supplements I suggest are just for optimal health and immunity, such as vitamin D, omega-3 fatty acids, and probiotics. Other supplements, such as iron, iodine, calcium, and zinc are included on the list because the vegan diet is at a higher risk of deficiency in these minerals. These minerals can in fact be obtained by the vegan diet and are only listed as suggestions of levels to be aware of. Macro-nutrients, such as protein, do not need to be supplemented, but can be, to ensure adequate levels especially for athletes. Those wary of taking supplements or concerned about meeting their RDA may find comfort in getting their nutrient profile analyzed in a blood test to help them discern which supplements are necessary for them.

• Calcium. Vegans consuming too little calcium should consider taking a supplement to reach at least 525mg per day. However, it has been said around the vegan community that vegans require less calcium than omnivores because they are not using this mineral to neutralize the acidity produced by meat.

• Iodine. Crucial for healthy thyroid function, which controls metabolism. Vegans are considered at risk of iodine deficiency. Vegans not getting enough iodine from seaweed or iodized salt should consider taking a supplement.

• Iron. Essential for energy production and oxygen transportation. Because vegans are not consuming red meat rich in heme iron, they may be at risk of iron deficiency, especially people who menstruate, due to their monthly blood loss. I recommend talking to your doctor and getting your iron levels checked before supplementing, as consuming too much iron can have more adverse effects than consuming too little. Consuming a diet rich in plant-based, nonheme iron, along with vitamin C, and avoiding caffeine should suffice.

• Omega-3 Fatty Acids. Beneficial for brain and heart health, omega-3 fatty acids are high in diets rich in fatty fish such as salmon and sardines. However, vegans can skip the middleman and reach their RDA of omega-3 fatty acids by supplementing with algae oil.

• Probiotics. If you are not consuming fermented vegetables daily, I recommended taking a probiotic daily to increase the number of good bacteria in your gut.

• Raw Vegan Protein Powder. A vegan protein powder supplement can be added to smoothies to increase the amount of protein and calories, allowing for a more nutrient-dense, balanced, and satisfying breakfast. It's also great for athletes who want to repair muscle fibers.

• Vitamin B12. Although our gut bacteria makes vitamin B12, vegetarian diets are very low in this vitamin that is necessary for energy production and protein metabolism, so a supplement is highly recommended on the vegan diet.

• Vitamin D3 + K2. Essential for immunity. Because the sun makes vitamin D in our bodies, most people should supplement at least during the winter months, but it is more beneficial to take it all year.

• Zinc. Vegans are also at risk of being low in zinc, a mineral necessary for metabolism, immunity, and cell repair. Those vegans unable to reach the zinc RDA should first focus on adding zinc-rich foods into their diets before considering taking a supplement.

2 YOUR RAW VEGAN KITCHEN

Setting up your raw vegan kitchen may seem overwhelming to start, but think about it this way: You're adding years to your life! Eating fully raw vegan can be as simple or complex as you like. You can start with nothing more than a chef's knife and a cutting board, or you can load up your kitchen with all the fun tools and gadgets. Either way, once you learn how amazing it feels to nourish yourself with whole, living foods, you will never go back to an energy-depleting processed diet again. This chapter provides you with tips and tricks to get you started on the right foot.

TIPS FOR SETTING UP

As you get more accustomed to and involved in raw vegan cuisine, you will develop your own tricks of the trade that will make life easier for you. To get you started, here are some tips that I use when organizing my kitchen to set myself up for the most efficient and effective use of my time and money.

Buy Bulk

When stocking up on nuts, seeds, legumes, grains, dried fruit, herbs, spices, and powders, go for the bulk section! You can save a lot of money by buying bulk, so hit up your favorite big box store to load up. It's much cheaper to buy loose dried herbs than to pay for those tiny, over-priced jars.

Save Your Jars

When you finish up with your glass nut and seed butter jars, save them! Wash and store them to reuse when stocking your pantry. You want to get into the habit of storing your food in glass containers, and reusing old jars is a great way to save money. I like to soak them in soapy water and peel off the labels.

Look Ahead

Each week, look ahead and check out the week's meal plan and shopping lists. Wrap your head around what the coming week will look like and what you need to pick up fresh and prep at home. Follow the daily step-by-step instructions for meal prepping, soaking, sprouting, and dehydrating so you're organized and ready to go. The meal plan is designed to use up all the groceries, so there is little to no waste, saving you money.

Shop Organic, Local, and in Season

Buy organic when possible and check the Environmental Working Group's (EWG) Dirty Dozen and Clean Fifteen lists, updated yearly. Support your local farmers' markets and stock up every week with fresh produce, or join an organic CSA (community-sponsored agriculture, which delivers fresh produce to you weekly). On average, it costs about the same as the grocery store, but the tastes, colors, and textures are incomparable. Farmers' markets are also always fresh and in season, so you know you're getting the highest-quality nutrition, as opposed to produce shipped across the world and held in atmosphere-controlled environments. Whatever you do, buy products that are unsprayed and labeled non-GMO (note that all USDA-certified organic products are non-GMO by law), though many farmers who sell at farmers' markets use different certifications, as USDA organic certification is extremely expensive to obtain. Just ask the farmers about their farming practices, so you make sure you're getting the best food you can put into your body! Also, please assume that all the recipes in this book are calling for non-GMO, organic, or unsprayed produce.

Storing Your Produce

Bag your greens to keep them fresh. Spray them with a little water, put them in plastic food storage bags, and twist the tops to keep the moisture in. Tropical fruits, including avocados, do better on the counter at room temperature so they can ripen properly. More perishable produce like berries, greens, cucumbers, bell peppers, and cauliflower should be kept in your refrigerator's crisper drawers. For bunches of fresh herbs, cut a little bit off the stems, then place them in a jar of water, like with cut flowers, and store them in the refrigerator. Change the water every couple of days. For celery, wash it, cut it up, and store the stalks in a bowl of filtered water or like you would herbs, standing up in a jar of water.

THE RAW VEGAN PANTRY

Stocking your raw vegan pantry can be a process, so start slowly. Don't feel like you have to get every ingredient on this list right away, but preparation is key. My advice is to follow the meal plan and grab the ingredients listed for Week 1. That's a great place to start.

Nuts

To lengthen the shelf life of nuts, store in glass jars in the refrigerator or freezer. High-fat products will go rancid if stored in light or warm places.

Almonds	**Hazelnuts**	**Walnuts**
Brazil nuts	**Pecans**	
Cashews	**Pine nuts**	

Seeds

As with nuts, seeds should be stored in glass jars in the refrigerator or freezer.

Pumpkin	**Hemp**	**Sunflower**
Chia	**Sesame**	
Flax	**Sprouts**	

Legumes

Legumes should be purchased dried and then soaked and sprouted. Do not soak and sprout kidney beans or black beans, as they should not be eaten raw, hence why I left them off the list below.

Lentils: brown, green, and red	**Beans: chickpeas (garbanzo beans), adzuki**	**Peas: black-eyed peas, green (split)**

Grains and Flours

Purchase in bulk and store in the pantry.

Almond meal	**Quinoa**	**Rolled oats, gluten-free**
Almond flour	**Quinoa flour**	**Steel-cut oats, gluten-free**
Buckwheat groats	**Raw cacao powder**	**Wild rice**
Coconut flour	**Raw carob powder**	
Psyllium husk powder		

Dried Fruit

These can also be purchased in bulk and stored in the pantry.

Apricots	**Figs**	**Raisins**
Currants	**Goji berries**	**Tomatoes, sun-dried**
Dates, pitted	**Peaches**	

Oils and Butters

Look for whole food-derived oils that are unprocessed and cold pressed. Be aware of expiration or use-by dates, as oils will go rancid. For nut and seed butters, look for only one ingredient and make sure it does not say "roasted." (The one ingredient would be the nut or seed. For example: "almonds," as opposed to "sugar, canola oil, roasted almonds." You want the ingredient list to just say almonds, and preferably raw almonds—not roasted.) Grab these oils and butters from a health food store to ensure you're getting the best quality.

Almond butter, raw	**Flaxseed oil, cold-pressed (keep refrigerated)**	**Sesame oil (keep refrigerated)**
Avocado oil		**Tahini or sesame butter (keep refrigerated)**
Coconut butter	**Olive oil, cold-pressed extra-virgin**	
Coconut oil, virgin, unrefined	**Peanut butter, raw**	

Herbs and Spices

These are best purchased in bulk and stored in your own labeled glass jars.

Cayenne pepper

Chili powder

Cinnamon

Coconut aminos or low-sodium soy sauce

Cumin

Garlic powder

Ginger powder

Italian herbs

Miso paste (soy or chickpea)

Onion powder

Oregano

Paprika

Peppercorns

Red pepper flakes

Rosemary

Turmeric

Salt (preferably pink Himalayan or Celtic sea salt)

Other

Algae (spirulina, chlorella)

Cacao nibs, raw

Coconut, shredded and unsweetened

Dulse flakes

Maple syrup, pure

Nutritional yeast

Jackfruit

Monk fruit or stevia extract (note that some people are allergic to stevia)

Peppermint extract, pure

Protein powder, vegan, raw

Vanilla extract, pure

SOAKING AND SPROUTING: PREPARING NUTS AND LEGUMES

Soaking nuts and sprouting legumes is the way we prepare our food on the raw vegan diet. The process of soaking removes anti-nutrients and enzyme inhibitors such as lectins and phytic acid, allowing the seed to sprout and increase digestibility. Sprouting enhances the level of vitamins, minerals, and enzymes, improving the food's nutritional value and further increasing its digestibility.

There are two kinds of sprouts: The first group is composed of the mature sprouts such as alfalfa, clover, broccoli, and radish, which are like green vegetables in composition and take five days to fully grow. The second group is composed of grains and legumes such as buckwheat, lentils, and chickpeas that are sprouted in one day.

The sprouting procedure for mature sprouts is as follows:

Place two tablespoons of sprouting seeds in a one-quart jar. For the top, use a sprouting lid or nylon mesh with an elastic band. Soak overnight with filtered water and in the morning, give it a good rinse, and drain. Invert the jar, then rinse and drain twice a day, morning and night. After five days you should have a full jar of sprouts! Place them by a window to catch the sun's rays so the little leaves turn green.

The sprouting procedure for grains and legumes:

Immerse the grains and legumes in filtered water for a certain number of hours (based on the following chart), drain, and rinse. If you don't have a sprouting tray, you can leave smaller seeds like quinoa and buckwheat in a stainless-steel mesh strainer, and the larger lentils and chickpeas in a colander. Rinse morning and night until you see tails forming. When you see little tails, aka sprouts, you know you're on the right track.

Avoid kidney beans and black beans on this diet. Sprouting them is toxic!

Soaking and Sprouting Quick Reference Table

FOOD	DRY MEASURE	SOAK TIME IN HOURS	GROWING TIME IN DAYS	APPROXIMATE YIELD
Adzuki beans	1 cup	24 to 36	3 to 5	3 cups
Alfalfa, clover, broccoli, radish	2 tbsp seeds	4 to 12	4 to 6	1-quart jar
Almonds	1 cup	12 to 15	1	1¾ cups
Amaranth	1 cup	Overnight	2 to 3	3 cups
Barley, hulled	1 cup	24	1 to 3	2 cups
Brazil nuts	1 cup	8 hours or overnight		1 cup, soaked only

FOOD	DRY MEASURE	SOAK TIME IN HOURS	GROWING TIME IN DAYS	APPROXIMATE YIELD
Buckwheat, hulled	1 cup	30 minutes to overnight	1 to 2	2 cups
Chickpeas (Garbanzo beans)	1 cup	24 to 36	3	2½ cups
Dried fruit	1 cup	8 hours or overnight		1⅛ cups
Filberts	1 cup	12 to 15	1	1¼ cups
Flaxseed	¼ cup	Don't soak. Spray to keep moist.	3 to 5	2¾ cups
Lentils, green	1 cup	24	1 to 3	2¾ cups
Lentils, red	1 cup	8 hours or overnight	1	2¾ cups
Mung beans	1 cup	24 to 36	1 to 3	3¾ cups
Oat groats, hulled whole	1 cup	24	1 to 3	2¼ cups
Peas, whole dried	1 cup	24 to 36	2 to 4	2½ cups
Pine nuts	1 cup	8	8 hours or overnight	1¼ cups
Pumpkin seeds	1 cup	12 to 15	1 to 2	1½ cups
Quinoa	1 cup	24	1 to 2	2½ cups
Rice, brown (long/short grain)	1 cup	24 to 36	3 to 4	1½ cups
Rice, wild	1 cup	24 to 36	3 to 5	3 cups
Sesame seeds, unhulled	1 cup	12 to 15	1	2 cups
Soybeans	1 cup	24 to 36	3 to 4	2¾ cups
Sunflower seeds, hulled	1 cup	12 to 15	1 to 2	2 cups
Sunflower seeds, unhulled	3 cups	24	2	5 cups
Urad dal	1 cup	24	1 to 2	3½ cups

FREEZE IT!

Freezing food is one of the easiest forms of food preservation, and although food will safely keep in the freezer indefinitely, that doesn't mean it will retain its quality forever—the flavor and texture will decline with time, so try to consume within the optimal freezing time frame as shown in the following table.

Frozen vegetables bought at the grocery store are flash-steamed or blanched (dipped in boiling water) before frozen. The intention is to preserve color, retain vitamins, and reduce enzyme activity. However, that means they are no longer considered raw and cannot be used on the raw food diet. The higher the water content of a vegetable, the faster it crystallizes and the softer it becomes when thawed. The reason is that water expands when frozen, rupturing the plant cell wall, which is apparent by the mushy texture when thawed. Therefore, vegetables are best consumed fresh on the raw food diet. If you notice your veggies start to wilt and you won't get to eating them in time, wash, chop, and freeze them instead of discarding them. That way, you can throw them in your smoothies, blended soups, or even use them in your crackers!

Rule of thumb: the higher the fat content, the longer it will last frozen; the higher the water content, the shorter it will last frozen. The best quality and greatest nutrients are retained when food is fresh, dry, frozen quickly, stored in airtight packages, and used within 6 to 12 months. Air and moisture are the biggest enemies of frozen food, so after washing, dry your produce well before freezing to keep ice crystals from forming. Remove as much air as possible from the freezer bag to prevent oxidation or "freezer burn."

Frozen Produce Quick Reference Table

ITEM	PREP	CONTAINER	KEEPS FOR
Apples, pears, stone fruit	Core and chop then lay flat on a parchment paper–lined pan in freezer	Freezer bag	4 months
Asparagus	Trim	Freezer bag	6 months

Continued

ITEM	PREP	CONTAINER	KEEPS FOR
Avocado	Remove rind and pit, chop, and lay separate on parchment paper–lined pan in freezer	Freezer bag	5 months
Bananas	Peel and freeze whole or chop	Freezer bag	8 months
Beets	Peel and freeze whole	Freezer bag	12 months
Berries	Lay flat on a parchment paper–lined pan in freezer	Freezer bag	6 months
Bell Peppers	Cut in half, core	Freezer bag	3–4 months
Broccoli	Cut into chunks	Freezer bag	12 months
Carrots	Trim ends, freeze whole or chopped	Freezer bag	12 months
Cauliflower	Cut into chunks	Freezer bag	12 months
Celery	Trim end, freeze whole or chopped	Freezer bag	6 months
Fresh nut milk	Freeze in ice cube trays then pop out when frozen	Freezer bag	6 months
Fresh vegetable juice	Juice and freeze immediately	Glass jar	12 months
Green beans	Arrange in a single layer on a parchment paper-lined pan in freezer	Freezer bag	12 months
Juicer pulp	Straight from juicer container to freezer	Freezer bag	8 months
Leafy greens	Dry well before freezing	Freezer bag	3–4 months
Lentils, sprouted	Dry well before freezing	Glass jar or freezer bag	12 months
Nut pulp	Straight from nut-milk bag to freezer	Freezer bag	8 months
Tomatoes	Freeze whole, chopped or puréed	Freezer bag	3–4 months
Zucchini	Chop	Freezer bag	8 months

KITCHEN EQUIPMENT

With a new way of eating comes new kitchen equipment and gadgets to play with. There will be lots of chopping as you increase the amount of fresh fruits and vegetables in your diet, so you want to prepare them with good-quality, sharp knives. To extend the life of your knives, avoid hard-surfaced cutting boards like glass, stone, and bamboo, as they wreak havoc on your blades. A wooden block works the best.

I use my high-speed blender, food processor, and nut-milk bag every day, and I couldn't live without my veggie spiralizer. We want to make vegetables fun and exciting, so playing with their shapes, colors, and textures really brings your plate to life. You can get away with just a vegetable peeler, but it will take a bit longer, so make sure it's a sharp one!

My life truly changed when I purchased my dehydrator. A whole new world of possibilities opened up in my raw food life, and there were no limitations to what I could make. I highly recommend you purchase a dehydrator! Crackers, cookies, granola, muffins, bagels, wraps, bread—you name it, you can prepare all your favorite comfort carbs! The beauty of making these comfort carbs with whole, plant-based foods is that your body will recognize the nutrients and tell you when to stop eating. No more eating an entire box of crackers and wondering what just happened.

Essential Equipment

Blender, high-speed	Mason jars	Paring knife
Chef's knife	Measuring spoons	Sieve, fine-mesh stainless steel
Colander	Microplane grater	Vegetable peeler
Cutting board	Mixing bowls	Vegetable spiralizer
Food processor	Nut-milk bag	

Optional Equipment

Citrus juicer	Ice cream scoop, spring-released, or a melon baller	Mandoline
Coffee grinder		Sprouting tray or sprouting lid
Dehydrator		
Electric juicer		

3 21 DAYS TO BETTER HEALTH

As the old saying goes, failing to plan is planning to fail. This rings true with eating healthy. Knowing that meal prep is important is great, but putting action behind that intention is where success happens. Meal planning is a strategy that will not only keep you organized and efficient but also keep your body well-fed and nourished at all times. Following this 21-day raw vegan meal plan will ensure your highest level of health and vitality while saving you precious time and money. Eliminating the guesswork for you, this plan provides detailed daily instructions, prep tips, and grocery lists so all you have to do is execute and witness the amazing changes to your health and happiness.

THE FIRST WEEK

Welcome to your first week on the raw vegan diet! This week has been designed to ease you into the world of plant-based nutrition with lots of fresh fruits, veggies, and of course nuts, seeds, and legumes. The third week is where more dehydrated foods are introduced. You can use the first week as an entry point to the raw vegan diet or as a way to switch up some of your current meals. I recommend going all-in for 21 days! They say that is how long it takes to create a new habit.

Start preparing for your first week by shopping on Sunday, or Day 0, and follow the instructions provided. Remember, organization is key when eating healthy and is especially important when eating raw and vegan. Check out the recipe tips for substitutions based on your own preferences and make sure to update your grocery list if you make any changes.

Week 1 Suggested Meal Plan

	BREAKFAST	SNACK	LUNCH	SNACK	DINNER
Day 1	Carrot Cake Overnight Oats (page 77)	Apple (1)	Carrot Ginger Lime Soup (page 92)	Chocolate Almond Energy Balls (2) (page 156)	Rainbow Pad Thai with Spicy Almond Sauce (page 118)
Day 2	Very Berry Delicious Smoothie (page 58)	Almonds (¼ cup)	Rainbow Pad Thai with Spicy Almond Sauce (page 118)	Cucumber (½) and Zucchini Hummus (page 150) (¼ cup)	Kale Caesar Salad (page 99) with Almond Rawmesan Cheese (page 141) and Carrot Ginger Lime Soup (page 92)
Day 3	Carrot Cake Overnight Oats (page 77) with Coconut Yogurt (page 70)	Strawberries (1 cup)	Waldorf Salad (page 103) with Carrot Ginger Lime Soup (page 92)	Chocolate Almond Energy Balls (2) (page 156)	Collard Wraps (page 120)

	BREAKFAST	SNACK	LUNCH	SNACK	DINNER
Day 4	Green Giant Smoothie Bowl (page 57)	Walnuts (¼ cup)	Cauliflower Tabouli Salad (page 104) and Collard Wraps (page 120)	Cherry Tomatoes (½ cup) and Zucchini Hummus (page 150) (¼ cup)	Fettuccine Alfredo (page 121) and Almond Raw-mesan Cheese (page 141)
Day 5	Citrus Fruit Salad (page 75) with Granola/Muesli (page 71) and Coconut Yogurt (page 70)	Grapes (1 cup)	Fettuccine Alfredo (page 121) and Almond Raw-mesan Cheese (page 141)	Chocolate Almond Energy Balls (2) (page 156)	Mediterranean Buddha Bowl with Seasoned Sprouted Chickpeas (page 106) and Zucchini Hummus (page 150)
Day 6	Very Berry Delicious Smoothie (page 58)	Pecans (¼ cup)	Mediterranean Buddha Bowl with Seasoned Sprouted Chickpeas (page 106)	Celery (2 stalks) and Almond Butter (2 tablespoons)	Creamy Tomato and Red Pepper Soup (page 93) with Lentil Almond Croutons (page 102), Almond Raw-mesan Cheese (page 141), and Cashew Cream (page 78)
Day 7	Citrus Fruit Salad (page 75) with Muesli / Granola (page 71) and Coconut Yogurt (page 70)	Raspberries (½ cup)	Creamy Tomato and Red Pepper Soup (page 93) with Seasoned Chickpeas (page 106), Lentil Almond Croutons (page 102), and Almond Raw-mesan Cheese (page 141)	Spicy Walnut Pâté Cucumber Boats (½ cucumber) (page 151)	Summer Citrus Salad (page 108)

Shopping List

FRUIT

- [ ] Apples, 5 (1 green)
- [ ] Bananas, 4
- [ ] Blueberries, 1 cup
- [ ] Grapefruit, 1
- [ ] Grapes, 3 cups or 1 bunch
- [ ] Kiwis, 3
- [ ] Lemons, 9
- [ ] Limes, 4
- [ ] Oranges, 4
- [ ] Raspberries, 1 cup
- [ ] Strawberries, 3 cups

VEGETABLES AND HERBS

- [ ] Alfalfa sprouts, 3 cups
- [ ] Avocados, 7
- [ ] Basil, 1 bunch
- [ ] Bell peppers, red, 5
- [ ] Bell peppers, orange, 2
- [ ] Cabbage, purple, 1
- [ ] Carrots, 11
- [ ] Cauliflower, 1 large or 4½ cups
- [ ] Celery, 1 bunch
- [ ] Cilantro, 1 bunch
- [ ] Collard leaves, 4
- [ ] Cucumbers, English, 4
- [ ] Garlic, 2 heads or 1 jar, pre-minced
- [ ] Ginger root, 1
- [ ] Jalapeño pepper, 1 large or 3 tablespoons
- [ ] Kalamata olives, ½ cup
- [ ] Kale, 1 bunch
- [ ] Mint, 1 bunch
- [ ] Onion, green, 1 bunch
- [ ] Onion, red, 1 small
- [ ] Onion, sweet, 1
- [ ] Parsley, 1 bunch
- [ ] Romaine lettuce, 4 cups or 1 head
- [ ] Spinach, 7 cups
- [ ] Tomatoes, cherry, 2½ cups
- [ ] Tomatoes, Roma, 2
- [ ] Tomatoes, sun-dried, 1 jar or 1 package
- [ ] Zucchini, 9

DRY BULK

- [ ] Almonds, 4 cups
- [ ] Buckwheat groats, hulled, 1 cup
- [ ] Cashews, 2 cups
- [ ] Cayenne pepper
- [ ] Chia seeds, ½ cup
- [ ] Chili powder
- [ ] Chickpeas, dried, 1 cup
- [ ] Cinnamon, ground
- [ ] Cocoa powder, ½ cup
- [ ] Coconut, unsweetened, shredded, 1 cup
- [ ] Coconut, unsweetened, large flakes, 1 cup
- [ ] Cumin
- [ ] Dates, pitted, 2 cups
- [ ] Flaxseed, ½ cup
- [ ] Garlic powder
- [ ] Ginger, ground
- [ ] Goji berries, ¼ cup
- [ ] Hemp seeds, 1½ cups
- [ ] Himalayan pink salt
- [ ] Italian herbs, dried
- [ ] Lentils, green, dried, 1½ cups
- [ ] Nutritional yeast, ½ cup
- [ ] Onion powder
- [ ] Oregano, dried
- [ ] Paprika
- [ ] Pecans, ½ cup
- [ ] Peppercorns
- [ ] Pine nuts, ¼ cup
- [ ] Pumpkin seeds, ¼ cup
- [ ] Raisins, ½ cup
- [ ] Rolled oats, gluten-free, large-flake, 3 cups
- [ ] Rosemary, dried
- [ ] Sunflower seeds, 1½ cups
- [ ] Thyme, dried
- [ ] Turmeric powder
- [ ] Walnuts, 3½ cups

OTHER

- [ ] Almond butter, raw
- [ ] Apple cider vinegar, raw
- [ ] Coconut milk, full-fat, 2 cans
- [ ] Coconut water (optional for smoothies)
- [ ] Garlic, pre-minced (optional if using fresh garlic)
- [ ] Kelp noodles
- [ ] Lime juice
- [ ] Liquid smoke
- [ ] Maple syrup, pure
- [ ] Miso paste
- [ ] Olive oil, extra-virgin
- [ ] Probiotic capsules, 1 bottle
- [ ] Protein powder, raw vegan (optional for smoothies)
- [ ] Soy sauce (low-sodium), or coconut aminos
- [ ] Tahini
- [ ] Vanilla extract, pure

Below is a list of daily prep instructions starting on Sunday or Day 0. Following these specific instructions will ensure optimal organization and success in this meal plan.

At the end of the week, look ahead at next week's grocery list and see if any leftover groceries can be used, such as herbs or celery. If not, leftover fruit, veggies, and herbs can be thrown into the blended soups, smoothies, infused water, or eaten as a snack. You will have leftover bulk ingredients, so be sure to account for that in the next week's grocery list. Note that you will need to keep the following from Week 1's groceries for Week 2: 1 cup of grapes, 1 celery stalk, ¼ cup parsley, and ¼ cup basil.

SUNDAY, DAY 0

♦ Grab groceries for Week 1.

♦ Soak 1 cup green lentils and 1 cup chickpeas for 24 hours.

♦ Soak 2 cups cashews and 2 cups almonds for 2 to 4 hours.

♦ Make Coconut Yogurt, leaving it somewhere warm to ferment for 12 to 24 hours.

♦ After a couple of hours of soaking, make Cashew Cream. You will use ½ cup in the Carrot Ginger Lime soup, ¼ cup in the Carrot Cake Overnight Oats, and refrigerate the rest in a glass jar for the Day 2 salad dressing.

♦ Make the Carrot Ginger Lime Soup. Divide into three glass jars and store in refrigerator.

♦ Make Chocolate Almond Energy Balls with ½ cup of the soaking almonds. Store in refrigerator or freezer.

♦ Make almond milk with the rest of the soaking almonds. Store in a glass jar in the refrigerator. Dehydrate the almond pulp overnight or store in refrigerator.

- Make two servings of Carrot Cake Overnight Oats. Store in two glass jars in the refrigerator.

MONDAY, DAY 1

- Now that the legumes have soaked for 24 hours, it's time to sprout! Transfer the green lentils and chickpeas to colanders (or a sprouting tray or a mesh bag also works). Rinse well and leave on the counter for a couple of days, rinsing morning and night until little sprouts form, probably by Wednesday, Day 3.

- The Coconut Yogurt should be ready after 12 to 24 hours of fermenting. Store in a lidded glass container in the refrigerator.

- If you opted for the purple cabbage when making the Rainbow Pad Thai, make sauerkraut with the leftover cabbage. The cabbage will be fine sitting for a week if you want to wait. Make lunch for Day 2.

- Make Zucchini Hummus.

- If you have a dehydrator, make Coconut Bacon for the Kale Caesar Salad dinner on Day 2.

TUESDAY, DAY 2

- Continue rinsing the legumes twice a day.

- While you're making Kale Caesar Salad for dinner, make Waldorf Salad for lunch Day 3. They both use the same dressing. Use the leftover Cashew Cream for the Kale Caesar Salad dressing. Leave the dressing on the side and mix in right before eating. Save the leftover Caesar dressing for wraps during Week 3; store it in your freezer.

- Make Almond Rawmesan Cheese for the salad.

- Soak 1 cup of buckwheat overnight.

WEDNESDAY, DAY 3

♦ In the morning, sprout buckwheat by rinsing it very well, then transfer it to a fine-mesh colander or cheesecloth. Leave it to sprout for 1 to 2 days, rinsing twice a day, until you see little tails.

♦ By now, the legumes should be ready. Transfer to a lidded glass container and store in the refrigerator. Chickpeas may take another day.

♦ Make Cauliflower Tabouli Salad for lunch Day 4 to enjoy with left-over Collard Wraps.

♦ Soak ¼ cup each of sunflower seeds, pumpkin seeds, goji berries, and raisins for Granola/Muesli.

THURSDAY, DAY 4

♦ Make Sunflower Seedballs, Almond Rawmesan Cheese, and Alfredo sauce for dinner. Pack a portion for lunch Day 5.

♦ Buckwheat should be ready. Make the muesli and stewed apple-sauce. If you have a dehydrator, mix the applesauce with the muesli and dehydrate overnight to make granola.

♦ Make Citrus Fruit Salad for breakfast Days 5 and 7 and dinner Day 7. Feel free to use up any leftover fruit in the fruit salad, such as the half green apple left over from the smoothie bowl. Leave 1 cup grapes for snack Day 8.

♦ Make the seasoned sprouted chickpeas. Dehydrate them if you prefer crunchy chickpeas.

FRIDAY, DAY 5

♦ If you have a dehydrator, make Lentil Almond Croutons. Or you can make them the morning of Day 6 to enjoy at dinner.

SATURDAY, DAY 6

♦ When making the Creamy Tomato and Red Pepper Soup, use up any leftover coconut milk. Garnish the tomato soup with Lentil Almond Croutons, Seasoned Sprouted Chickpeas, and any leftover Cashew Cream. Save two servings for lunch Days 7 and 8.

♦ Soak 1 cup quinoa for 24 hours.

♦ Soak 1 cup walnuts for Spicy Walnut Pâté Cucumber Boats.

♦ If making Savory Flax Crackers on Sunday, Day 7, soak ingredients overnight.

SUNDAY, DAY 7

♦ Grab groceries for Week 2.

♦ Make the Spicy Walnut Pâté Cucumber Boats. Make cucumber boats for snack Days 7 and 8 with 1 cucumber.

♦ Seal mesh over quinoa jar with elastic band. Drain and rinse. Invert quinoa jar in a glass container to sprout 1 to 2 days, rinsing twice a day.

♦ Soak 1 cup cashews overnight for Cashew Sour Cream.

♦ Soak ½ cup wild rice for 24 hours

♦ Soak ¾ cup green lentils for 24 hours.

♦ Soak 1 cup of Brazil nuts for 2 hours, then make Nutty Nut Milk.

♦ Make two servings of Chia Berry Breakfast Pudding.

♦ If you have a dehydrator, make the Oatmeal Raisin Cookies. If not, make the recipe into energy balls. Leave ½ cup of the batter aside to make the Oatmeal Raisin Smoothie for Day 9.

♦ Make Savory Flax Crackers. Use up any leftover vegetables.

THE SECOND WEEK

Congratulations on making it to Week 2! I bet you feel amazing! This week I have included a few more dehydrated options such as cookies and crackers. If you don't yet have a dehydrator, the Oatmeal Raisin Cookies can be made into Oatmeal Raisin Energy Balls. Another option is checking out your local health food store for raw, dehydrated crackers and wraps to enjoy the meal plan to its fullest potential.

Week 2 Suggested Meal Plan

	BREAKFAST	SNACK	LUNCH	SNACK	DINNER
Day 8	Chia Berry Breakfast Pudding (page 80)	Grapes (1 cup)	Creamy Tomato and Red Pepper Soup (page 93) with Spicy Walnut Pâté Lettuce Wraps (page 111)	Spicy Walnut Pâté Cucumber Boats (½ recipe) (page 151)	Raw Mexi Chili (page 95) with Cashew Sour Cream (page 113)
Day 9	Oatmeal Raisin Cookie Smoothie (page 53)	Pecans (¼ cup)	Raw Mexi Chili (page 95) with Cashew Sour Cream (page 113)	Oatmeal Raisin Cookies (2) (page 163)	Super Seed Power Bowl with Orange Ginger Dressing (page 109)
Day 10	Chia Berry Breakfast Pudding (page 80)	Pear (1)	Super Seed Power Bowl with Orange Ginger Dressing (page 109)	Snap peas (1 cup) and Guacamole (¼ cup) (page 149)	Lentil Walnut Tacos (page 124) with Mango Salsa (page 148), Guacamole (page 149), and Cashew Sour Cream (page 113)

	BREAKFAST	SNACK	LUNCH	SNACK	DINNER
Day 11	Green Beauty Smoothie (page 52)	Brazil nuts (¼ cup)	Lentil Walnut Taco Salad (page 112) with Mango Salsa (page 148), Guacamole (page 149), and Cashew Sour Cream (page 113)	Oatmeal Raisin Cookies (2) (page 163)	Watermelon Gazpacho (page 96) and Savory Flax Crackers (page 154)
Day 12	Fresh Fruit and Yogurt Parfait with Granola/ Muesli (page 74)	Apple (1)	Watermelon Gazpacho (page 96) and Savory Flax Crackers (page 154)	Veggies (1 cup) and Guacamole (¼ cup) (page 149)	Cauliflower Mash with Tahini Miso Gravy (page 126) and Caramelized Onions (page 128), and Sunflower Seedballs (page 122)
Day 13	Green Beauty Smoothie (page 52)	Walnuts (¼ cup)	Dragon Bowl with Tahini Miso Gravy (page 129)	Jicama Fries and Ketchup (page 155)	Raw Vegan Mac 'n' Cheese (page 130)
Day 14	Fresh Fruit and Yogurt Parfait with Granola/ Muesli (page 74)	Straw-berries (1 cup)	Raw Vegan Mac 'n' Cheese (page 130) with Jicama Fries and Ketchup (page 155)	Oatmeal Raisin Cookies (2) (page 163)	Dragon Bowl with Tahini Miso Gravy (page 129)

Shopping List

FRUIT

- [ ] Apples, 2
- [ ] Banana, 1
- [ ] Blueberries, 1 cup
- [ ] Grapes, 1 cup (from Week 1)
- [ ] Lemons, 4
- [ ] Limes, 4
- [ ] Mango, ½ cup
- [ ] Oranges, 2
- [ ] Peach, 1
- [ ] Pears, 2
- [ ] Pineapple, 2 cups
- [ ] Raspberries, 1 cup
- [ ] Strawberries, 2 cups
- [ ] Watermelon, 1

VEGETABLES AND HERBS

- [ ] Alfalfa sprouts, 1 cup
- [ ] Avocados, 6
- [ ] Baby kale, 2 cups
- [ ] Basil, ¼ cup (from Week 1)
- [ ] Bell peppers, red, 6
- [ ] Beets, 2
- [ ] Carrots, 4
- [ ] Cauliflower, 3 cups
- [ ] Celery, 1 stalk (from Week 1)
- [ ] Cilantro, 2 cups
- [ ] Corn, 1 cup
- [ ] Cucumbers, 2
- [ ] Garlic, 1 head
- [ ] Jalapeño pepper, 1 large
- [ ] Jicama, 1
- [ ] Onion, red, 1
- [ ] Onions, sweet, 2
- [ ] Parsley, ¼ cup (from Week 1)
- [ ] Romaine lettuce, 1 head
- [ ] Snap peas, 2 cups
- [ ] Spinach, 3 cups
- [ ] Tomatoes, cherry, 3 cups
- [ ] Tomatoes, Roma, 7
- [ ] Tomatoes, sun-dried, 1 cup
- [ ] Zucchini, green, 4
- [ ] Zucchini, yellow, 1

DRY BULK

- ☐ Brazil nuts, 1¼ cups
- ☐ Blueberries, dried, ¼ cup
- ☐ Cashews, 2¾ cups
- ☐ Chia seeds, ½ cup
- ☐ Coconut, shredded, unsweetened, ½ cup
- ☐ Dates, ¾ cup
- ☐ Flaxseed, 1¾ cups

- ☐ Hemp seeds, ½ cup
- ☐ Lentils, ¾ cup
- ☐ Nutritional Yeast, ½ cup
- ☐ Pecans, 1¼ cups
- ☐ Pine nuts, ¼ cup
- ☐ Pumpkin seeds, ¾ cup
- ☐ Psyllium husk powder, 2 teaspoons

- ☐ Raisins, ½ cup
- ☐ Rice, wild, ½ cup
- ☐ Rolled oats, gluten-free, large flake, 1½ cups
- ☐ Sunflower seeds, ¾ cup
- ☐ Quinoa, ½ cup
- ☐ Walnuts, 1¼ cups

OTHER

- ☐ Coconut milk, full fat, 2 cans

- ☐ Coconut water, 2 cups (optional for smoothies)

- ☐ Spirulina or chlorella (optional for smoothies)
- ☐ Tahini, ½ cup

MONDAY, DAY 8

 ◆ After 24 hours, drain and rinse the wild rice and green lentils. Sprout in colanders and continue to rinse twice a day. Wild rice will take 3 to 5 days to sprout.

 ◆ Quinoa should be finished sprouting after 24 hours. Store in the refrigerator in a lidded glass container.

 ◆ Make Guacamole and Cashew Sour Cream.

WEDNESDAY, DAY 10

 ◆ Lentils should be sprouted. Store in the refrigerator.

 ◆ Make Coconut Yogurt and leave in a warm place overnight to ferment for 12 to 24 hours.

THURSDAY, DAY 11

 ◆ Place the yogurt in a lidded glass container in the refrigerator.

 ◆ If you have a dehydrator, make Caramelized Onions.

FRIDAY, DAY 12

 ◆ Soak 1½ cups of cashews to make the cheese sauce for Raw Vegan Mac 'n' Cheese and Cheesy Kale Chips.

 ◆ The wild rice should be sprouted. Make two servings of Dragon Bowls for lunch on Day 13 and dinner on Day 14.

 ◆ Make Jicama Fries and Ketchup for your snack on Day 13 and lunch Day 14.

SUNDAY, DAY 14

♦ Get groceries for Week 3.

♦ Soak seeds for Italian Onion Bread for 2 hours before making, if you have a dehydrator.

♦ Make Banana Flax Crepes in the dehydrator, if you have one.

♦ Make Cheesy Kale Chips (with the cheese sauce from Mac 'n' Cheese) in the dehydrator.

♦ Make two servings of Rainbow Salad in a Jar with Berry Vinaigrette for lunch Days 15 and 17.

♦ Soak 1½ cups cashews for ¾ cup Dill Cashew Cream Cheese, ½ cup Sun-Dried Tomato Sauce, and ¼ cup Cashew Dream Cream.

♦ For the granola bars and pizza crust, which require a dehydrator, soak 1½ cups buckwheat. Sprout buckwheat after 8 hours of soaking.

♦ Make hemp milk.

THE THIRD WEEK

You've made it to Week 3! For this week, there are even more dehydrated options. I have included fresh alternatives such as lettuce wraps instead of butternut squash wraps, trail mix instead of granola bars, oats instead of crepes, a smoothie instead of bagels, and leftovers instead of pizza.

I have included the ingredients for both the fresh and dehydrated options in the shopping list, so make sure to adjust as necessary.

Week 3 Suggested Meal Plan

	BREAKFAST	SNACK	LUNCH	SNACK	DINNER
Day 15	Taste of the Tropics Smoothie (page 60)	Pear (1)	Rainbow Salad in a Jar with Berry Vinaigrette (page 114)	Cheesy Kale Chips (1½ cups) (page 152) or Jicama Fries and Ketchup (page 155)	Sprouted Lentil Stew with Spanish Cauliflower Rice (page 132) and Italian Onion Bread (page 135)
Day 16	Stewed Applesauce (page 72) and Cashew Dream Cream (page 79) with Banana Flax Crepes (page 82) or Classic Overnight Oats (page 76)	Walnuts (¼ cup)	Sprouted Lentil Stew with Spanish Cauliflower Rice (page 132)	Veggies (1 cup) and Dill Cashew Cream Cheese (page 88) (2 T)	Jackfruit Sloppy Joes (page 134)
Day 17	Apple Pear Ginger Smoothie (page 61)	Raspberries (½ cup)	Rainbow Salad in a Jar with Berry Vinaigrette (page 114)	Sprouted Buckwheat Granola Bars (page 158) or Raw Trail Mix (page 159) (¼ cup)	Raw Lasagna with Basil Pesto and Brazil Nut Ricotta (page 136)

	BREAKFAST	SNACK	LUNCH	SNACK	DINNER
Day 18	Stewed Apple-sauce (page 72) and Cashew Dream Cream (page 79) with Banana Flax Crepes (page 82) or Classic Overnight Oats (page 76)	Almonds (¼ cup)	Raw Lasagna with Basil Pesto and Brazil Nut Ricotta (page 136)	Veggies (1 cup) and Dill Cashew Cream Cheese (page 88) (2 T)	Creamy Avo-cado Pesto Pasta (page 140) with Sunflower Seedballs (page 122)
Day 19	Taste of the Tropics Smoothie (page 60)	Apple (1)	Butternut Squash Veggie-Wrapped Veggies (page 142) with Dill Cashew Cream Cheese (page 88), or Collard Wraps (page 120)	Sprouted Buckwheat Granola Bar (page 158) or Raw Trail Mix (page 159) (¼ cup)	Cauliflower Mash with Tahini Miso Gravy (page 126) and Italian Onion Bread (page 135)
Day 20	Coco Banana Smoothie (page 55)	Pecans (¼ cup)	Rainbow Pad Thai with Spicy Almond Sauce (page 118)	Veggies (1 cup) and Dill Cashew Cream Cheese (page 88) (2 T)	Creamy Avo-cado Pesto Pasta (page 140) with Sunflower Seedballs (page 122)
Day 21	Loaded Everything Bagel with Dill Cashew Cream Cheese (page 86)	Black-berries (½ cup)	Butternut Squash Veggie-Wrapped Veggies (page 142) with Dill Cashew Cream Cheese (page 88), or Collard Wraps (page 120)	Real Fruit Leather (page 157) or Berries (½ cup) with Cashew Dream Cream (page 79) (1 T)	Raw Vegan Pizza (page 144) or leftovers

Shopping List

FRUIT

- ☐ Apples, 5
- ☐ Bananas, 10
- ☐ Blackberries, 1 cup
- ☐ Blueberries, 1 cup

- ☐ Lemons, 3
- ☐ Lime
- ☐ Mango, 1 cup
- ☐ Pears, 2

- ☐ Pineapple, 1 cup
- ☐ Raspberries, 3 cups

VEGETABLES AND HERBS

- ☐ Alfalfa sprouts, 1 cup
- ☐ Avocados, 5
- ☐ Basil, 1 bunch (1½ cups)
- ☐ Beet
- ☐ Butternut squash, 2½ cups
- ☐ Carrots, 5
- ☐ Cauliflower, 1 head (2 cups)
- ☐ Celery, 2 stalks
- ☐ Cucumber

- ☐ Dill, 1 bunch
- ☐ Garlic, 4 cloves
- ☐ Jackfruit
- ☐ Kale, 1 bunch
- ☐ Parsley, ¼ cup
- ☐ Red bell pepper, 3
- ☐ Roma tomatoes, 11
- ☐ Romaine lettuce, 1 head (only if you have no dehydrator and need to use lettuce wraps)

- ☐ Spinach, 2 bunches or 1 large pre-washed container (approximately 8 cups)
- ☐ Sun-dried tomatoes, 1¼ cups
- ☐ Sweet onions, 2
- ☐ Yellow bell pepper
- ☐ Zucchini, 9

DRY BULK

- [ ] Almonds, 2 cups
- [ ] Brazil nuts, ¾ cup
- [ ] Buckwheat groats, 1¾ cups
- [ ] Cacao nibs, ¼ cup
- [ ] Cashews, 3 cups
- [ ] Chia seeds, 2 tablespoons
- [ ] Cocoa powder, 1 tablespoon
- [ ] Dates, ¾ cup

- [ ] Flaxseed, 4 cups
- [ ] Green lentils, ¾ cup
- [ ] Goji berries, ¼ cup
- [ ] Hemp seeds, 1¼ cups
- [ ] Nutritional yeast, ⅓ cup
- [ ] Pecans, 2 cups
- [ ] Pine nuts, ¾ cup
- [ ] Psyllium husk powder, ¾ cup
- [ ] Pumpkin seeds, ¼ cup

- [ ] Quinoa flour, 1 cup
- [ ] Raisins, ¼ cup
- [ ] Rolled oats, gluten-free, large flake, 2¼ cups
- [ ] Sunflower seeds, 1½ cups
- [ ] Unsweetened shredded coconut, ¾ cup
- [ ] Walnuts, ¾ cup

OTHER

- [ ] Coconut milk, full-fat, 1 can
- [ ] Coconut water, 2 cups (optional for smoothies)

- [ ] Jackfruit in water, 1 can (if not found in produce section)
- [ ] Vinegar, balsamic

MONDAY, DAY 15

- Rinse buckwheat twice today.

- Make ¾ cup Dill Cashew Cream Cheese and ¼ cup Cashew Dream Cream.

- Make two servings of Classic Overnight Oats if not making crepes.

- Make Stewed Applesauce for crepes or oats.

- When preparing the Sprouted Lentil Stew with Spanish Cauliflower Rice, double the recipe of Sun-Dried Tomato Sauce. It will also be used in the Jackfruit Sloppy Joes, Raw Lasagna with Basil Pesto and Brazil Nut Ricotta, and Raw Vegan Pizza.

- Soak appropriate ingredients for Sprouted Buckwheat Granola Bars if you have a dehydrator.

TUESDAY, DAY 16

- The buckwheat will be ready for the granola bars if you have a dehydrator. If not, make Raw Trail Mix.

- For your snack, use a half cucumber and any leftover veggies from recipes.

WEDNESDAY, DAY 17

- Pesto from Raw Lasagna with Basil Pesto and Brazil Nut Ricotta will also be used in Creamy Avocado Pesto Pasta for dinner on Days 18 and 20.

THURSDAY, DAY 18

- Make butternut squash wraps for Butternut Squash Veggie-Wrapped Veggies if you have a dehydrator. If not, use romaine lettuce wraps or make Collard Wraps for lunch on Days 19 and 20.

SATURDAY, DAY 20

♦ Make bagels, pizza crust, and fruit roll-ups if you have a dehydrator.

SUNDAY, DAY 21

♦ Use up ingredients from Raw Lasagna with Basil Pesto and Brazil Nut Ricotta on Raw Vegan Pizza, such as the tomato sauce, pesto, Almond Rawmesan Cheese, Brazil Nut Ricotta, etc.

♦ If you don't have a dehydrator to make bagels and pizza crust, use up leftover fruit and veggies to make a smoothie, lettuce wraps, and a salad.

♦ If you don't have a dehydrator to make fruit roll-ups, have fresh berries with Cashew Dream Cream.

RAW AND VEGAN FOR LIFE

Let me be the first to congratulate you on completing the 21 days as a raw, vegan foodie. Not only have you developed a new plant-based habit, but also your health and energy levels have most likely improved immensely. Whether you can see the changes externally or not, know that benefits do exist internally. Now what? Where do you go from here?

If you find yourself slipping back into your old, detrimental eating habits, I assure you that your body will let you know immediately through stomach pains, bloating, diarrhea, constipation, brain fog, exhaustion, and/or skin breakouts. The cleaner you eat for longer, the sooner and more intense the effects will be when you don't. If you do experience any of those symptoms, use it as an opportunity to identify any food intolerances. Listen to your body and pay attention to the signs; if you don't feel good, then you shouldn't be eating that food. I encourage you to stay the course and continue to nourish your body with whole, plant-based living foods. Keep the momentum going and ride the wave of feeling good.

Check out the resources at the end of this book and take note of the websites, blogs, books, and schools that will keep you in the know and motivated. There is a wealth of raw vegan recipes online and cookbooks for sale that will keep you inspired. Eating out has never been easier or more convenient for us health nuts—raw and vegan restaurants are popping up all over the place, especially in major cities and health-conscious towns. Most traditional restaurants offer fresh salads, and even fast-food joints are jumping on the bandwagon and offering plant-based options. Bring hemp hearts, nuts, and seeds in your bag and add them to restaurant salads for extra protein. Health food stores are gold mines for raw, vegan foods and often have delicious salad bars and delis to eat at.

Your local health food store will also supply you with necessary supplements. Talk to your doctor about getting your bloodwork checked so you know if there is anything specific you need to take such as iron or vitamin B12. As a general rule, I recommend my clients take vitamin D, omega-3, probiotic, and vitamin B12 (if they are vegetarian or vegan).

Don't be too concerned about going 100 percent raw 100 percent of the time. Again, if you can eat raw 75 percent of the time, that's great! Just be conscious about what you eat and focus on how it nourishes you, as opposed to being obsessed with perfection and worried about a label. All you can do is your best.

Taste of the Tropics
Smoothie, page 60

SATISFYING SMOOTHIES

MAKE YOUR OWN SMOOTHIE

Smoothies are a great way to ease yourself into the world of plant-based living foods. There are so many variations and flavors you can play around with. Smoothies are also a great way to sneak powerful superfoods, healing herbs, and extra veggies into your diet. All that is required is a high-speed blender and a little preparation. Try out my favorite smoothie recipes listed below or build your own!

Smoothies can be made into smoothie bowls by adding just enough liquid to blend into a thick and creamy texture. The toppings are the best part of smoothie bowls! You can top your smoothie bowl with granola, crushed nuts, hemp seeds, chia seeds, cacao nibs, coconut flakes, berries, or fresh fruit slices and enjoy it with a spoon.

If you would like a thicker smoothie, use less liquid or add ice; a thinner smoothie, add more liquid. You can use any liquid you have on hand for the smoothie such as nut milk, coconut water, or filtered water. For a balanced meal, make sure to include a fat such as half an avocado, a high-fiber carbohydrate in the form of fruits and vegetables, and a protein such as hemp seeds or peanut butter. Most importantly, have fun with it!

1. Pick one base.

☐ Pure water   ☐ Coconut water   ☐ Hemp milk

☐ Infused water   ☐ Nut milk, unsweetened

☐ Fresh vegetable juice   ☐ Coconut milk

2. Pick one fat. *Use 1 to 2 tablespoons.*

☐ Flax oil   ☐ Nut butter

☐ Avocado (use one half)   ☐ Seed butter

☐ Coconut oil or butter

3. Pick one or two fruits—use two small handfuls of each, fresh or frozen.

☐ Banana*　　　　☐ Nectarine/Peach*　　　☐ Pear

☐ Berries　　　　☐ Apple　　　　　　　☐ Kiwi*

☐ Cherries　　　☐ Plum　　　　　　　☐ Pineapple

☐ Lemon/Lime　　☐ Watermelon*

☐ Mango*　　　　☐ Cantaloupe*

*Soluble-fiber fruits provide a smoother overall finish to your smoothie.

4. Pick two or three vegetables—use one heaping handful of each vegetable choice.

☐ Leafy greens (baby spinach, baby kale, romaine lettuce, collard greens)

☐ Cucumber　　　☐ Cilantro

☐ Celery　　　　☐ Parsley

☐ Zucchini　　　☐ Basil

☐ Cauliflower　　☐ Mint

5. Optional

♦ *Pick one superfood.*

☐ Hemp seeds, 1 to 2 tablespoons

☐ Raw cacao powder, 1 to 2 tablespoons

☐ Goji berries, 1 to 2 tablespoons

☐ Maca powder, 1 to 2 teaspoons

☐ Chia seeds, 1 to 2 tablespoons

☐ Turmeric powder, ¼ to ½ teaspoon

☐ Ground flaxseed, 1 to 2 tablespoons

☐ Spirulina or chlorella, 1 to 2 teaspoons

♦ *Pick one supplement or spice.*

☐ Cinnamon, ¼ teaspoon

☐ Raw vegan protein powder, 1 scoop

☐ Oatmeal, 1 to 2 tablespoons

☐ Vanilla, 1 teaspoon

☐ Greens powder, 1 to 2 teaspoons

☐ Ginger, ½ teaspoon

☐ Cardamom, ¼ teaspoon

♦ *Pick one sweetener*

☐ Maple syrup, 1 to 2 teaspoons

☐ Soaked dates, 1 to 2

GREEN BEAUTY SMOOTHIE

YIELD: 1 serving

If you're new to smoothies, feel free to just stick to spinach in your green smoothies as the taste is undetectable. Also, if you don't have a high-speed blender like a Vitamix, you might want to stick to softer greens, like spinach and baby kale, as chard and mature kale don't blend very easily in a standard blender.

1 cup water or coconut water

½ banana, frozen

½ cup chopped pineapple, frozen

Small handful spinach

Small handful baby kale

Juice of ½ lemon

1 pitted date, soaked 20 minutes

1 tablespoon ground flaxseed

1 teaspoon spirulina or chlorella

Blend ingredients until smooth and enjoy!

VARIATION TIP: Feel free to add a raw, vegan protein powder to your smoothie to increase your protein intake.

Per serving: Calories: 188; Total fat: 4g; Sodium: 43mg; Carbohydrates: 38g; Fiber: 7g; Sugar: 22g; Protein: 6g

OATMEAL RAISIN COOKIE SMOOTHIE

YIELD: 1 serving

When you're making the Oatmeal Raisin Cookies recipe (page 163), save a little of the batter for a delicious filling smoothie to start your day off. It's also a great post-workout meal to replenish those glycogen stores or even a yummy afternoon treat when you're craving that cookie. The ice cubes are essential to make this smoothie cold, thick, and creamy.

1 cup nut milk of choice

½ cup Oatmeal Raisin Cookies batter (page 163)

3 to 5 ice cubes

Blend ingredients until smooth and enjoy!

VARIATION TIP: For a creamier and thicker smoothie, add a frozen banana.

Per serving: Calories: 381; Total fat: 22g; Sodium: 174mg; Carbohydrates: 41g; Fiber: 8g; Sugar: 20g; Protein: 9g

IMMUNE BOOSTER SMOOTHIE

YIELD: 1 serving

This is a great smoothie for those winter months when that nasty cold and flu bug is lurking around. Supporting your immune system is your best defense. Vitamin C–packed citrus and antioxidant-rich blueberries unite with immune-boosting ginger to create an army that no bug can stand against. For additional support, spirulina is another powerhouse full of antioxidants and protein, maca provides extra energy, and cayenne will clear out those sinuses while boosting your metabolism.

2 medium seedless navel oranges, peeled

½ cup blueberries

2 tablespoons fresh lemon juice

1 to 2 teaspoons ginger, peeled and grated, to taste

1 teaspoon spirulina (optional)

1 teaspoon maca (optional)

Pinch cayenne pepper (optional)

Blend ingredients until smooth and enjoy!

VARIATION TIP: Add hemp seeds, avocado, or nut butter for healthy fat to keep you fuller for longer.

Per serving: Calories: 172; Total fat: <1g; Sodium: 11mg; Carbohydrates: 43g; Fiber: 8g; Sugar: 32g; Protein: 3g

COCO BANANA SMOOTHIE

YIELD: 1 serving

An all-time favorite. This classic chocolate banana smoothie will satisfy anyone's chocolate craving while providing total body nourishment at the same time.

1 frozen banana

1 cup almond milk

1 tablespoon almond butter

1 tablespoon cocoa powder

1 tablespoon ground flaxseed

1 teaspoon vanilla extract

Small pinch Himalayan pink salt

3 or 4 ice cubes

Blend ingredients until smooth and enjoy!

VARIATION TIP: Try adding ¼ teaspoon espresso powder and call it a mocha!

Per serving: Calories: 323; Total fat: 16g; Sodium: 155mg; Carbohydrates: 44g; Fiber: 9g; Sugar: 23g; Protein: 7g

RESCUE ME SMOOTHIE

YIELD: 1 serving

After a grueling workout at the gym, this is not only a great recovery smoothie but also a great reward! It will be sure to replenish your glycogen stores and rebuild those broken muscle fibers. The peanut butter adds fat and protein.

1 cup almond milk

2 tablespoons gluten-free rolled oats

2 dates, pitted, soaked 30 minutes in water

1 tablespoon raw peanut butter

1 tablespoon chia seeds

¼ teaspoon ground cinnamon

¼ teaspoon vanilla extract

¼ teaspoon turmeric powder

Pinch Himalayan pink salt

4 or 5 ice cubes

Blend ingredients until smooth and enjoy!

VARIATION TIP: If you wish to increase the protein content of this smoothie, feel free to top it up with raw vegan protein powder.

Per serving: Calories: 319; Total fat: 14g; Sodium: 211mg; Carbohydrates: 36g; Fiber: 10g; Sugar: 19g; Protein: 10g

GREEN GIANT SMOOTHIE BOWL

YIELD: 1 serving

You can make any smoothie into a smoothie bowl but the creamier the ingredients the better. That's why a whole frozen banana and avocado are added to this recipe. Celery adds additional nutrients and a bit of a crunch, stimulating healthy digestion, which starts in the mouth. Think of chewing as the first step to a healthy gut.

For the Smoothie

Handful spinach

1 kiwi

1 frozen banana

½ avocado

½ celery stalk

½ green apple

1 tablespoon hemp seeds

1 scoop vegan protein powder (optional)

¼ cup coconut water

For the toppers

Coconut flakes

Cacao nibs

Raw granola

Hemp seeds

Fresh fruit pieces

Nuts and seeds

1. Blend ingredients until smooth, adding liquid slowly to create a thick smoothie texture that can be eaten with a spoon.

2. Pour into a bowl, add toppers, and enjoy!

Per serving: Calories: 425; Total fat: 19g; Sodium: 75mg; Carbohydrates: 65g; Fiber: 16g; Sugar: 36g; Protein: 8g

VERY BERRY DELICIOUS SMOOTHIE

YIELD: 1 serving

You can't go wrong with berries. Full of antioxidants, vitamins, and fiber, berries are among the healthiest foods on the planet. The richer the color, the more powerful the antioxidants from phytonutrients.

1 cup almond milk

½ cup strawberries

¼ cup blueberries

¼ cup raspberries

½ avocado

Handful baby spinach

1 tablespoon hemp seeds

Blend ingredients until smooth and enjoy!

VARIATION TIP: Switch out the avocado for banana for extra sweetness while keeping the same creamy texture.

Per serving: Calories: 295; Total fat: 21g; Sodium: 203mg; Carbohydrates: 24g; Fiber: 13g; Sugar: 9g; Protein: 8g

BLUEBERRY AVOCADO DREAM SMOOTHIE

YIELD: 1 serving

I was thinking about calling this smoothie "Your Daily Dose of Fiber" but that didn't sound as smooth and sleek as "Blueberry Avocado Dream." You wouldn't think so by looking at them, but avocados are packed full of fiber. Just one avocado has 13 grams of dietary fiber! And you thought they were all fat, didn't you? This smoothie provides 16 grams of fiber, which is an impressive start to the day when aiming for 30 grams of total fiber.

1 cup almond milk

1 cup blueberries

½ frozen banana

½ avocado

1 tablespoon almond butter

1 tablespoon ground flaxseed

Blend ingredients until smooth and enjoy!

INGREDIENT TIP: If the smoothie is too thick, add more liquid.

Per serving: Calories: 441; Total fat: 28g; Sodium: 188mg; Carbohydrates: 48g; Fiber: 15g; Sugar: 23g; Protein: 8g

TASTE OF THE TROPICS SMOOTHIE

YIELD: 1 serving

Take me to the beach! Just the aroma of the tropical fruit blending brings me back to the tropical paradise where the smoothie bar sat nestled between a banana tree and a coconut tree. Now that is fresh! The hint of ginger and the zing of lime provide the perfect balance to the sweet tropical fruit. And don't forget your protein! Hemp seeds pack a powerful protein punch.

1 cup coconut water or water

½ cup mango

½ cup pineapple

½ frozen banana

Handful spinach

1 tablespoon lime juice

1 tablespoon hemp seeds

1 teaspoon fresh ginger, peeled and grated

¼ teaspoon turmeric powder

Blend ingredients until smooth and enjoy!

VARIATION TIP: This is a great smoothie to make into a smoothie bowl. Leave the liquid out, add the ingredients to the blender, and add a little bit of liquid at a time until a smoothie bowl consistency is reached.

Per serving: Calories: 261; Total fat: 5g; Sodium: 73mg; Carbohydrates: 51g; Fiber: 6g; Sugar: 37g; Protein: 6g

APPLE PEAR GINGER SMOOTHIE

This smoothie reminds me of home in the Okanagan, where apple and pear orchards are on every corner. A perfect fall smoothie when harvest season is in full bloom and the fruits are at peak deliciousness. The creamy avocado and tart ginger add texture and flavor to this heartwarming apple and pear combo.

1 cup water

1 pear

½ green apple

½ avocado

Handful baby spinach

1 tablespoon hemp seeds

2 teaspoons fresh ginger, peeled and grated

¼ teaspoon cinnamon

Blend ingredients until smooth and enjoy!

VARIATION TIP: Add any liquid you like. Almond milk would go well with this smoothie.

Per serving: Calories: 333; Total fat: 18g; Sodium: 32mg; Carbohydrates: 43g; Fiber: 15g; Sugar: 26g; Protein: 7g

Infused Waters

A lot people struggle with drinking enough water. They know it's good for their health and even beneficial for their weight-loss goals, but for some, it isn't appetizing and more of a chore than anything. Infused water is a great way to enjoy your daily eight glasses, as the slices of fresh fruits and veggies not only give the water a sweet and aromatic flavor, but also add vitamins, antioxidants, and alkalizing effects.

I like to use a large glass jug with a narrow spout to catch the fruit when pouring out the water. Planning ahead and letting the infusion do its work overnight will do wonders for your morning glass of water. Since you can't squeeze the juice out of a berry like you can a lemon, letting the berries infuse in the water to release their flavors and nutrients will take time, but it is well worth the wait. Remember, you can always eat the fruit after or throw it in your smoothie.

You can choose a variety of fresh or frozen fruits, berries, citrus, veggies, and herbs to add to a quart of filtered water. Let it sit and infuse for at least an hour. The flavor will get stronger and the color will get brighter as time goes on. Try the recipes in the following chart or be creative and try a combination of your own choosing.

INGREDIENTS ADD TO 1 QUART OF FILTERED WATER	INFUSION TIME OVERNIGHT WORKS GREAT FOR A TASTY GLASS OF WATER IN THE MORNING
1 cup sliced strawberries, 1 sliced cucumber, large handful fresh basil	Overnight
1 sliced cucumber, large handful fresh mint	1 hour to overnight
1 sliced kiwi, 1 cup blueberries, 1 orange (sliced or squeezed)	Overnight
1 cup sliced pineapple, 1 sliced cucumber, small handful fresh mint	Drink immediately or infuse overnight
1 cup mixed berries, 1 lemon (sliced or squeezed), 1 sliced cucumber, small handful fresh basil	Drink immediately or infuse overnight
1 cup raspberries, 1 lime (squeezed), 1 cucumber sliced	Drink immediately or infuse overnight
1 cup sliced strawberries, 1-2 lemons (sliced or squeezed), 1 small handful fresh rosemary	Overnight
1 grapefruit (squeezed), 1 lemon (squeezed)	Drink immediately
2 sliced oranges, 1 sliced lemon, small handful fresh mint	Drink immediately or infuse overnight
1 to 2 cups mixed blackberries, blueberries, and raspberries	Overnight
1 sliced lemon, 1 sliced lime, large handful cilantro	Drink immediately or infuse overnight
½ medium watermelon blended and strained of pulp, large handful fresh basil, large handful fresh mint	Drink immediately or infuse overnight

Nutty Nut Milk,
page 66

5 BOUNTIFUL BREAKFASTS

NUTTY NUT MILK

PREP TIME: 5 minutes, plus soaking time | YIELD: 2½ cups

Homemade nut milks are fast and easy to make. What's more, they actually taste like nuts! Commercial nut milks are full of fillers and additives to prevent them from separating and to add thickness. One such additive is the infamous carrageenan, which has a bad reputation for causing inflammation and digestive problems. Protect your guts and blend your nuts! Brazil nut milk would be a great choice for those with thyroid issues as they are an excellent source of selenium.

Suggested Equipment: **High-speed blender, Nut-milk bag**

1 cup almonds, cashews, Brazil nuts, or hazelnuts, soaked overnight (soaking optional)

2½ cups water

1 teaspoon vanilla extract

1 soaked date, ½ teaspoon of maple syrup, or 1 to 2 drops liquid monk fruit extract (optional)

1. Blend nuts in a high-speed blender with water for at least 30 seconds.

2. Pour into a bowl through a nut-milk bag. Squeeze and twist to get all the liquid out.

3. Add the vanilla and sweetener (if using).

4. Store in a glass jar in the refrigerator and plan to consume within 5 days.

INGREDIENT TIP: The leftover pulp from making nut milk can be reused. Cashew pulp can be used in smoothies or soups. Almond pulp can be dehydrated overnight and ground into almond flour.

VARIATION TIP: After you've made nut milk a few times, you can play around with the ratio of water to nuts, depending on your preference. I personally like my nut milk on the creamier side.

Per serving (½ cup almond milk): Calories: 170; Total fat: 14g; Sodium: <1mg; Carbohydrates: 8g; Fiber: 4g; Sugar: 2g; Protein: 6g

INSTANT HEMP MILK

PREP TIME: 2 minutes | **YIELD:** 2 cups

Hemp seeds, also known as hemp hearts, have a mild, nutty flavor and are nutrient powerhouses. This milk is made in an instant as no soaking or straining is required. High in protein and fat, hemp seeds also contain a healthy dose of calcium, magnesium, phosphorus, and potassium.

Suggested Equipment: **High-speed blender**

¼ cup hulled hemp seeds

2 cups water

1 teaspoon vanilla extract

1 soaked date, or ½ teaspoon of maple syrup or 1 to 2 drops liquid monk fruit extract (optional)

1. Blend hemp seeds and water in a high-speed blender for at least 30 seconds.

2. Add vanilla and sweetener (if using).

3. Refrigerate in a glass container and plan to consume within 5 days.

VARIATION TIP: Depending on your preference, you can play with the ratio of water to hemp seeds. I personally like my hemp milk on the creamier side.

Per serving (1 cup): Calories: 119; Total fat: 9g; Sodium: <1mg; Carbohydrates: 2g; Fiber: 2g; Sugar: <1g; Protein: 7g

CULTURED CASHEW YOGURT

PREP TIME: 5 minutes, plus soaking and fermenting time | YIELD: 2 cups

This cultured cashew yogurt is thick, tangy, delicious, and filled with good-for-the-gut probiotic cultures. It's a breeze to make and is a perfect addition to the Raw Muesli Power Bowl (page 71) or Stewed Apple Granola (page 72). It can be enjoyed topped with fresh fruit or berries, or added to smoothies and soups for additional creaminess.

Suggested Equipment: **High-speed blender**

2 cups cashews

1½ cups warm purified water

2 capsules or ¼ teaspoon probiotic powder

1. Soak cashews in enough water to cover for 1 to 2 hours or overnight. Drain and rinse after soaking.

2. Add cashews and warm water to blender and blend until smooth.

3. Transfer to a sterilized glass jar or bowl. You can sterilize by rinsing it with boiling water and letting it dry completely. Once it has cooled to room temperature, add ingredients. (Sterilizing the bowl isn't completely necessary if crunched for time.)

4. Add the contents of two probiotic capsules to the cashew cream. Use a wooden or plastic spoon to mix; a metal spoon can react negatively with the probiotics.

5. Cover with a light towel, cheesecloth, or loose lid—something that will keep the bugs out but allows air in. Secure the towel or cloth with a rubber band.

6. Place in a warm location for 12 to 24 hours to ferment. If your house is cold, find a warm place such as on top of the refrigerator, close to a heater, on a heating pad, etc. This will speed up fermentation.

7. When it has formed into a thick curd with a layer of liquid on the bottom, transfer to the refrigerator. Chill for at least 1 hour. When ready to eat, stir the layers together.

8. Stored in a sealed glass container in the refrigerator, it will keep for 1 week.

VARIATION TIP: If you want a sweeter yogurt or a vanilla flavor, add vanilla extract and maple syrup to your preferred flavor and sweetness. You can also divide the yogurt in two and have one plain and one flavored.

Per serving (1 cup): Calories: 786; Total fat: 64g; Sodium: 22mg; Carbohydrates: 45g; Fiber: 4g; Sugar: 7g; Protein: 21g

COCONUT YOGURT

PREP TIME: 5 minutes, plus fermenting time | YIELD: 2 cups

If you like the taste of coconut, you will love this yogurt. I make this yogurt all the time, because it is so easy and I love how creamy and tangy it is. Its high fat content makes it satisfying and filling so a little goes a long way.

1 can full-fat coconut milk

2 capsules or ¼ teaspoon probiotic powder

1. Empty the can of coconut milk into a bowl. Make sure the milk and cream are completely mixed (see tip). If not, blend and pour it back into the bowl.

2. Add the contents of 2 probiotic capsules to the coconut cream. Use a wooden or plastic spoon to mix; a metal spoon can react negatively with the probiotics.

3. Cover with a light towel, cheesecloth, or a loose lid—something that will keep the bugs out but allows air in. Secure the towel or cloth with a rubber band.

4. Place in a warm location for 12 to 24 hours to ferment. If your house is cold, find a warm place such as on top of the refrigerator, close to a heater, or on a heating pad. This will speed up fermentation.

5. When it has fermented, transfer to the refrigerator. Chill for at least 1 hour. When ready to eat, give it a stir.

6. Store in a sealed glass container in the refrigerator for up to 1 week.

INGREDIENT TIP: Before opening, shake the can of coconut milk vigorously to combine the cream with the water inside.

VARIATION TIP: If you want a sweeter yogurt or a vanilla flavor, add vanilla extract and maple syrup to your preferred flavor and sweetness. You can also divide the yogurt in two and have one plain and one flavored.

Per serving (1 cup): Calories: 352; Total fat: 35g; Sodium: 50mg; Carbohydrates: 5g; Fiber: 0g; Sugar: 3g; Protein: 3g

RAW MUESLI POWER BOWL

This is a hearty breakfast full of clean energy to keep you going all morning. It's super handy to have around, and it lasts a long time in the refrigerator or freezer, so double or triple this recipe! It can be enjoyed with nut milk topped with fresh fruit or berries or as a parfait with tangy Coconut Yogurt (page 70). The walnuts are a great source of omega-3 fatty acids and the hemp seeds are protein powerhouses.

2 cups gluten-free rolled oats

1 cup walnuts, chopped

½ cup sprouted buckwheat groats

½ cup shredded coconut, unsweetened

¼ cup sunflower seeds, soaked

¼ cup pumpkin seeds, soaked

¼ cup goji berries

¼ cup raisins, soaked

¼ cup chia seed

¼ cup hemp seeds

½ teaspoon cinnamon

¼ teaspoon Himalayan pink salt

Optional add-ins: cacao nibs, sprouted quinoa, dried apricots (soaked), or dried blueberries (soaked)

1. Sprout buckwheat groats according to sprouting instructions (pages 18–20).

2. Soak sunflower seeds and pumpkin seeds in 1 cup warm water overnight.

3. Soak goji berries together with raisins in ½ cup warm water overnight.

4. Combine all ingredients in a large bowl.

5. Top with fresh fruit and serve with nut milk.

INGREDIENT TIP: These ingredients can be purchased in bulk to save money. You can make the muesli any way you like by adding more options or leaving some out.

VARIATION TIP: I like to take half of this recipe and add stewed applesauce, then dehydrate it overnight for a yummy crunchy granola in the morning. I keep the other half as raw muesli.

Per serving: (½ cup) Calories: 297; Total fat: 18g; Sodium: 72mg; Carbohydrates: 28g; Fiber: 7g; Sugar: 5g; Protein: 10g

STEWED APPLE GRANOLA

PREP TIME: 20 minutes, plus dehydrating time | YIELD: 6 cups

A delicious topper for a smoothie bowl, it can also be enjoyed alone with fresh nut milk or cashew yogurt. It's always good to add a fresh element such as fresh fruit or berries to balance the dry element. Make a large batch on a Sunday and enjoy it all week. It can also be enjoyed as a satisfying afternoon snack!

Suggested Equipment: **High-speed blender, Dehydrator**

For the applesauce

2 apples, cored and chopped

2 bananas

1 cup water

½ cup raisin/goji soaking water if available, or plain water

1 teaspoon cinnamon

½ teaspoon ground ginger

¼ teaspoon Himalayan pink salt

For the granola

4 cups stewed applesauce

5 cups raw muesli

To make the applesauce

Add apples, bananas, water, spices, and salt to a high-speed blender and blend until well combined.

To make the granola

1. Pour the stewed applesauce into a bowl. Add muesli and mix until the muesli is well coated with the applesauce.

2. Spread the mixture onto nonstick dehydrator sheets or parchment paper and dehydrate for 8 to 12 hours, or overnight. Break the mixture up into pieces and dehydrate for another 4 hours, or until completely dry.

3. Store in an airtight container.

VARIATION TIP: The stewed applesauce can be made with any fruit you like. Try making sauce from peaches or pears; or replace the banana with mango! It can also be eaten as is, like applesauce, or mixed in with the raw muesli if you don't have a dehydrator.

Per serving (½ cup): Calories: 181; Total fat: 9g; Sodium: 3mg; Carbohydrates: 23g; Fiber: 5g; Sugar: 7g; Protein: 5g

FRESH FRUIT AND YOGURT PARFAIT WITH GRANOLA/MUESLI

PREP TIME: 10 minutes | YIELD: 2 servings

The best part about parfaits are that they are easy to put together, especially if you have premade granola and yogurt on hand. Sweet and tangy flavors coupled with creamy and crunchy textures make a parfait so tasty, it can even be enjoyed as dessert!

1 nectarine or peach, pitted and chopped

1 pear or apple, cored and chopped

½ cup fresh strawberries, stemmed and sliced

½ cup fresh blueberries or berry of choice

1 cup Granola (page 72) or Muesli (page 71)

1 cup Coconut Yogurt (page 70)

In two parfait glasses or bowls, layer fruit, berries, granola or muesli, and yogurt, and repeat in that order until all ingredients are used up.

VARIATION TIP: Choose any fresh or frozen fruits or berries you prefer to layer in your parfait.

Per serving: Calories: 591; Total fat: 36g; Sodium: 33mg; Carbohydrates: 60g; Fiber: 13g; Sugar: 26g; Protein: 13g

CITRUS FRUIT SALAD

PREP TIME: 10 minutes | **YIELD**: 3 servings (makes 4 cups)

Citrus fruits are not only flavorful and pretty, they're also good for you. Full of vitamin C, this salad strengthens your immunity and is full of antioxidants. Try it alongside Blueberry Muffin Tops (page 85)!

2 oranges, peeled and sliced

2 kiwi, peeled and sliced

1 red grapefruit, peeled and sliced

1 cup grapes, halved

1 cup strawberries, stemmed and sliced

½ cup blueberries

Mix all the fruit together in a large bowl and enjoy!

VARIATION TIP: Try adding the citrus fruit salad to a green salad for lunch.

Per serving: Calories: 150; Total fat: 1g; Sodium: 5mg; Carbohydrates: 38g; Fiber: 8g; Sugar: 25g; Protein: 2g

CLASSIC OVERNIGHT OATS

PREP TIME: 5 minutes | YIELD: 2 servings

This is one of my favorite go-to breakfasts. Prepare a couple of jars before bed and you're all set for a grab-and-go breakfast in the morning. Gluten-free whole-grain oats are a great source of fiber, vitamins, and minerals, such as vitamin B1 and manganese.

1½ cups nut milk

1 ripe banana, mashed

¾ cup gluten-free rolled oats

1 tablespoon chia seeds

2 tablespoons hemp seeds

1 teaspoon vanilla extract

¼ teaspoon cinnamon

Pinch Himalayan pink salt

Berries and crushed nuts (for topping)

1. Mix the nut milk, banana, oats, chia seeds, hemp seeds, vanilla, cinnamon, and salt together in a bowl.

2. Place into two Mason jars or other individual lidded glass containers.

3. Cover and refrigerate overnight.

4. Top with crushed nuts and berries before serving.

VARIATION TIP: There are endless variations of overnight oat flavors. Try adding raw peanut butter and cacao powder for a peanut butter chocolate flavor, or kiwi and mango for a tropical flavor.

Per serving: Calories: 311; Total fat: 12g; Sodium: 130mg; Carbohydrates: 41g; Fiber: 11g; Sugar: 9g; Protein: 12g

CARROT CAKE OVERNIGHT OATS

PREP TIME: 10 minutes | YIELD: 2 servings

Carrot cake is my favorite flavor of overnight oats. It's like having cake for breakfast! I recommend opting for gluten-free rolled oats over regular oats, regardless if you have sensitivity to gluten or not, in order to avoid a low-grade inflammatory response in your body.

1½ cups nut milk

1 ripe banana, mashed

1 large carrot, shredded

¾ cup gluten-free rolled oats

¼ cup raisins

¼ cup Cashew Cream (page 78)

1 tablespoon chia seeds

2 tablespoons hemp seeds

2 teaspoons maple syrup (optional)

1 teaspoon vanilla extract

½ teaspoon cinnamon

Pinch Himalayan pink salt

Pecan pieces, for topping

Raisins, for topping

Shredded carrot, for topping

1. Mix the nut milk, banana, carrot, oats, raisins, Cashew Cream, chia seeds, hemp seeds, maple syrup (if using), vanilla, cinnamon, and salt together in a bowl.

2. Place into two Mason jars or other individual lidded glass containers.

3. Cover and refrigerate overnight.

4. Top with pecan pieces, raisins, and shredded carrot before serving.

VARIATION TIP: If you don't have cashews on hand to soak and prepare Cashew Cream, you can add another raw vegan yogurt or coconut cream instead. The chia seeds and hemp seeds add nutritional value, but are not necessary to prepare the oats. Feel free to omit them or substitute an equivalent amount of other healthy seeds.

Per serving: Calories: 501; Total fat: 21g; Sodium: 160mg; Carbohydrates: 68g; Fiber: 14g; Sugar: 24g; Protein: 15g

CASHEW CREAM

PREP TIME: 5 minutes | YIELD: 1¾ cups

Cashew Cream has so many uses and can be made in 5 minutes! Use as a base for vegan mayonnaise, yogurt, cheese sauce, cream cheese, sour cream, sweet cream, or to thicken soups. The possibilities are endless!

2 cups raw cashews soaked overnight   **¼ to ½ cup water**

1. Blend cashews with ¼ cup of water in a high-speed blender until smooth and creamy. If needed, add more water a tablespoon at a time to blend.

2. Store in a lidded glass container in the refrigerator for 5 days.

VARIATION TIP: See all the different cashew recipes for all the possibilities that start with Cashew Cream.

Per serving (¼ cup): Calories: 225; Total fat: 18g; Sodium: 6mg; Carbohydrates: 13g; Fiber: 1g; Sugar: 2g; Protein: 6g

CASHEW DREAM CREAM

PREP TIME: 5 minutes | YIELD: 1 cup

This sweet version of Cashew Cream can be used as the finishing touch or creamy base for any sweet dish. Spread it on Banana Flax Crepes (page 82) or Real Fruit Leather (page 157) or enjoy it with fresh berries.

Suggested Equipment: **High-speed blender**

1 cup Cashew Cream (page 78)

1 tablespoon maple syrup

1 teaspoon vanilla extract

1. Blend all ingredients in a high-speed blender until smooth and creamy.

2. Store in a lidded glass container in the refrigerator for 5 days.

VARIATION TIP: If you want to limit your sugar intake, replace the maple syrup with a few drops of monk fruit extract.

Per serving (¼ cup): Calories: 241; Total fat: 18g; Sodium: 7mg; Carbohydrates: 17g; Fiber: 1g; Sugar: 5g; Protein: 6g

CHIA BERRY BREAKFAST PUDDING

PREP TIME: 5 minutes | YIELD: 2 servings

If you love berries, you will love this recipe. Bursting with berry flavors, this chia breakfast pudding can be made ahead of time for a delicious and nutritious grab-and-go breakfast. Chia seeds have become one of the most popular superfoods in the health community. These tasty seeds are easy to digest and high in protein, omega-3s, manganese, and antioxidants.

1½ cups nut milk

1 cup coconut milk

½ cup chia seeds

1 tablespoon maple syrup

1 teaspoon vanilla extract

½ cup blueberries

½ cup raspberries

Crushed nuts, coconut flakes, and cacao nibs (for topping)

1. In a bowl, combine the nut milk, coconut milk, chia seeds, maple syrup, and vanilla. Divide into 2 lidded glass containers.

2. Cover and refrigerate for 2 hours or overnight.

3. Serve with berries and toppings.

VARIATION TIP: Choose any combination of your favorite berries and nuts.

Per serving: Calories: 542; Total fat: 35g; Sodium: 161mg; Carbohydrates: 39g; Fiber: 24g; Sugar: 13g; Protein: 15g

BANANA OATMEAL PANCAKES

PREP TIME: 30 minutes, plus dehydrating time | YIELD: 10 pancakes

These raw pancakes are hearty and filling, yet soft and pliable. Flavored with bananas, orange juice, vanilla, and a hint of cinnamon, your kitchen is going to smell heavenly! Prepare them after dinner and they should be ready for breakfast.

Suggested Equipment: **Dehydrator**

5 ripe bananas, chopped finely	**Juice of 1 fresh orange**
¾ cup gluten-free rolled oats	**½ teaspoon cinnamon**
¼ cup flaxseed, ground	**½ teaspoon vanilla extract**

1. Add all ingredients to a bowl and mix until thoroughly combined.

2. Scoop ⅓ cup batter onto nonstick dehydrator sheets and shape into pancakes. Four can fit on one sheet. If you have a ring mold, you can use that to carefully fill and shape your pancakes.

3. Dehydrate at 115°F for 12 to 18 hours. They are ready when they are soft, but dry enough so you can peel them off the dehydrator sheets or parchment paper.

PREPARATION TIP: Try serving your pancakes with a berry compote. Pulse a cup of thawed berries in a blender until well mixed. Pour over the pancakes and serve.

Per serving (1 pancake): Calories: 186; Total fat: 4g; Sodium: 2mg; Carbohydrates: 38g; Fiber: 6g; Sugar: 16g; Protein: 4g

BANANA FLAX CREPES

PREP TIME: 30 minutes, plus dehydrating time | YIELD: 8 to 12 crepes

I love this recipe. It's quick and easy to prepare, super healthy, and a family favorite. Once the crepes are done, the filling options are endless. My favorite is peaches and cream!

Suggested Equipment: **High-speed blender, Dehydrator**

¾ cup flaxseed, ground	**½ cup coconut, shredded**
3 bananas	**1 teaspoon vanilla**
1 cup zucchini	**¼ teaspoon cinnamon**

1. Grind the flaxseed in a high-speed blender or grinder until fine.

2. Add all the ingredients to the blender and blend until smooth.

3. Take ⅓ cup of the batter and place in all four corners of a nonstick dehydrator sheet or parchment paper.

4. Use a small offset spatula to form batter into four 6-inch disks that are ¼ inch thick.

5. Dehydrate at 115°F for 5½ hours. Be sure to respect the time so they don't dry out.

6. Flip and dehydrate for 30 minutes longer, until dry to the touch.

7. Store in the refrigerator in a zip-top bag to keep soft.

VARIATION TIP: Roll up these crepes with your favorite fruit or berries and nut butter, Cashew Dream Cream (page 79), or Whipped Coconut Cream (page 84).

Per serving (1 crepe): Calories: 129; Total fat: 8g; Sodium: 3mg; Carbohydrates: 15g; Fiber: 4g; Sugar: 6g; Protein: 3g

PEACHES AND CREAM CREPES

PREP TIME: 10 minutes | YIELD: 2 servings

This is such a dreamy, creamy crepe recipe. Perfectly delicate and tender, these crepes will melt in your mouth and leave you coming back for more.

Suggested Equipment: **Dehydrator, Hand mixer, High-speed blender**

4 Banana Flax Crepes (page 82)

1 cup Whipped Coconut Cream (page 84)

3 fresh peaches, thinly sliced, divided

1. Lay crepes out flat. Spread them with a generous layer of whipped cream and line slices of two of the fresh peaches down the middle of the crepes. Roll up and pin with a toothpick to keep the roll in place.

2. Add the third peach to the blender and blend into a sauce. Add a bit of water if needed.

3. Drizzle the rolled-up crepes with the peach sauce and serve.

VARIATION TIP: Instead of the peach sauce, squeeze fresh lemon juice on the crepes and sprinkle with cinnamon. If you want a creamier and sweeter peach sauce, add half of a fresh banana to the blender with the peach.

Per serving: Calories: 609; Total fat: 44g; Sodium: 40mg; Carbohydrates: 54g; Fiber: 11g; Sugar: 30g; Protein: 9g

WHIPPED COCONUT CREAM

PREP TIME: 10 minutes, plus overnight chilling | YIELD: 1½ cups

This is a whipped cream that is perfect for topping desserts or serving with fresh berries. If you're like me, just eat it right out of the bowl!

Suggested Equipment: **Hand mixer**

1 (14-ounce) can full-fat coconut milk, chilled for at least 8 hours

½ teaspoon vanilla extract

1 to 2 tablespoons maple syrup, ¼ cup icing sugar, or 4 drops monk fruit extract

1. Chill a large mixing bowl for 10 minutes.

2. Remove coconut milk from refrigerator, being careful not to tip or shake the can to maintain separation of cream and liquid.

3. Scoop out the hardened coconut cream, leaving the liquid behind, and place in the chilled bowl.

4. Beat for 30 seconds with a mixer until creamy. Then add the vanilla and sweetener. Continue to mix until creamy and smooth, about 1 more minute.

5. Use immediately or refrigerate. Will keep for up to 1 to 2 weeks! It is not freezer friendly.

PREP TIP: I don't like my whipped cream too sweet, so I recommend adding the sweetener of your choosing a little at a time until the desired sweetness is reached.

Per serving (¼ cup): Calories: 144; Total fat: 14g; Sodium: 17mg; Carbohydrates: 4g; Fiber: 0g; Sugar: 3g; Protein: 1g

BLUEBERRY MUFFIN TOPS

PREP TIME: 10 minutes, plus dehydrating time | YIELD: 10 servings

These little muffins make a great snack and are easy to travel with. This recipe is a great way to use up that almond pulp from making almond milk. Serve with a dollop of almond butter or with a fresh fruit and yogurt parfait. They make a great grab-and-go snack for running out the door.

Suggested Equipment: **Dehydrator, Food processor**

2 cups almond flour

1 cup pecan pieces

¼ cup ground flaxseed

¼ cup psyllium husk powder

¼ cup liquid coconut oil

8 dates

1 tablespoon maple syrup

1 tablespoon almond milk

1 teaspoon vanilla extract

Pinch Himalayan pink salt

1 cup blueberries, fresh or frozen

1. Process all the ingredients except the blueberries until well combined.

2. Fold in blueberries.

3. Shape into 10 round patties and place directly on the dehydrator grate.

4. Dehydrate at 118°F for 3 hours, flip, and continue for 3 more hours until dry.

INGREDIENT TIP: If you don't have psyllium husk powder, you may substitute ground flaxseed. You can omit the maple syrup if desired, as the dates are sweet enough. However, if you don't have dates, use double the maple syrup. If you don't have almond flour, gluten-free oat flour will work instead.

Per serving: Calories: 311; Total fat: 26g; Sodium: 3mg; Carbohydrates: 19g; Fiber: 8g; Sugar: 8g; Protein: 7g

LOADED EVERYTHING BAGEL WITH DILL CASHEW CREAM CHEESE

PREP TIME: 30 minutes, plus dehydrating time | YIELD: 10 bagels

This recipe takes a little bit more time but is definitely worth the effort! The light and fluffy texture with a moist middle and crispy outside make these bagels a perfect home for all your favorite sandwich toppings.

Suggested Equipment: **Dehydrator, High-speed blender**

1 cup ground hazelnuts or almonds	¼ cup nutritional yeast
1 cup quinoa flour	2 tablespoons coconut butter
1 cup almond flour or oat flour	2 tablespoons olive oil
2 tablespoons psyllium husk powder	1 tablespoon maple syrup
1 tablespoon onion powder	1 tablespoon apple cider vinegar
1 teaspoon garlic powder	1 cup water
1 teaspoon Italian herbs	Dill Cashew Cream Cheese (page 88)
¼ teaspoon Himalayan pink salt	Freshly ground black pepper
1 cup zucchini or 1 medium zucchini, peeled	Fresh tomato slices, arugula, avocado slices, and alfalfa sprouts, for topping

1. Grind nuts in a high-speed blender or food processor. Oat flour can be made the same way.

2. In large bowl, combine the ground hazelnuts, quinoa flour, almond or oat flour, psyllium husk powder, onion powder, garlic powder, herbs, and salt until well mixed.

3. In a high-speed blender, blend the zucchini, nutritional yeast, coconut butter, olive oil, maple syrup, apple cider vinegar, and water until smooth.

4. Add the wet ingredients to the dry ingredients. Mix well to combine. Let stand for 5 minutes to thicken.

5. Form the mixture into 2-inch balls and then flatten until 1 inch thick. Make holes in the middle to suggest the shape of a bagel half.

6. Dehydrate on nonstick dehydrator trays or parchment paper for 6 to 8 hours at 115°F. Remove the trays or parchment paper and continue to dehydrate for 30 minutes to dry the bottoms.

7. Spread with a thick layer of cream cheese and top with black pepper, tomato slices, arugula, avocado, and alfalfa sprouts.

8. Bagels can be stored in a sealed container in the refrigerator. They will keep for 2 weeks.

VARIATION TIP: These bagels will also be a perfect base for Jackfruit Sloppy Joes (page 134) or to soak up any sauce left over from the Sprouted Lentil Stew with Spanish Cauliflower Rice (page 132).

Per serving (Two bagel halves without toppings): Calories: 236; Total fat: 16g; Sodium: 7mg; Carbohydrates: 19g; Fiber: 7g; Sugar: 3g; Protein: 8g

DILL CASHEW CREAM CHEESE

PREP TIME: 10 minutes | YIELD: 1 cup

Gut-friendly, probiotic-rich cashew cream cheese is a great addition to raw vegan bagels or can be enjoyed as a dip for fresh veggies.

Suggested Equipment: **High-speed blender**

1 cup cashews, soaked 20 minutes

¼ cup warm water

1 probiotic capsule

1 teaspoon onion powder

½ teaspoon garlic powder

¼ teaspoon Himalayan pink salt

1 to 2 tablespoons fresh chopped dill

1. Blend cashews and ¼ cup of warm water in a high-speed blender until smooth. Add contents of probiotic capsule and blend again to mix well.

2. Transfer to a bowl, cover and leave in a warm place for 8 to 12 hours to ferment. (It is ready when you see small air bubbles and it tastes slightly sour).

3. Once fermented, mix in the onion powder, garlic powder, and salt. Add dill to taste.

4. Store in an airtight glass container in the refrigerator for up to 5 days.

VARIATION TIP: Omit the dill for a cream cheese base you can flavor any way you like! I love swapping in sun-dried tomatoes to mix things up!

Per serving (2 tablespoons): Calories: 100; Total fat: 8g; Sodium: 3mg; Carbohydrates: 6g; Fiber: 1g; Sugar: 1g; Protein: 3g

Watermelon Gazpacho,
page 96, and Cauliflower
Tabouli Salad, page 104

6

SPLENDID SOUPS AND SALADS

CARROT GINGER LIME SOUP

Blended soups are a great way to use up veggies from your refrigerator. For example, if you have an overripe tomato or half a zucchini, throw it in! The cashews add creaminess, the avocado adds healthy fats, hemp seeds are high in protein, and the veggies provide fiber to the soup. It's a complete and balanced meal full of anti-inflammatory properties. Remember to garnish your blended soup with all your favorite fixings!

Suggested Equipment: **High-speed blender**

2 cups warm water, plus more as needed	**1 tablespoon miso paste**
4 large carrots, chopped	**1 tablespoon grated peeled ginger**
1 zucchini, chopped	**1 tablespoon olive oil**
1 garlic clove, minced or pressed	**1 teaspoon onion powder**
1 avocado	**1 teaspoon cumin**
Juice of 1 lime	**¼ teaspoon Himalayan pink salt**
½ cup freshly squeezed orange juice	**¼ teaspoon turmeric**
½ cup Cashew Cream (page 78)	**¼ teaspoon cinnamon**
¼ cup hemp seeds	**¼ teaspoon thyme**

Blend all ingredients in a high-speed blender. Start with the 2 cups of warm water and add more as needed to get desired consistency. Add more seasoning to your taste preference.

INGREDIENT TIP: Play around with the seasoning to get your desired flavor. Coconut aminos or tamari can replace the miso paste if needed.

Per serving: Calories: 454; Total fat: 32g; Sodium: 266mg; Carbohydrates: 34g; Fiber: 10g; Sugar: 12g; Protein: 12g

CREAMY TOMATO AND RED PEPPER SOUP

PREP TIME: 15 minutes | YIELD: 3 servings

This sweet and savory soup is a delicacy on a cold winter's evening. Adding a dollop of Cashew Cream to this soup transforms it into a luxurious creamy soup. With the creamy texture taken care of, make sure to garnish it with crunchy Lentil Almond Croutons (page 102) and add a fresh element of raw red pepper slices or fresh basil leaves. Blended soups are great for using up the veggies from your refrigerator. Just throw them in!

Suggested Equipment: **High-speed blender**

3 red bell peppers, divided
(2 whole and 1 diced)

2 ripe Roma tomatoes

1 yellow zucchini or peeled green zucchini

1 avocado

1 large carrot

Juice of 1 lemon

¼ cup oil-packed sun-dried tomatoes, drained

5 tablespoons hemp seeds, divided

1 tablespoon jalapeño pepper, minced

2 teaspoons minced peeled ginger

2 teaspoons cumin

1 teaspoon minced garlic

½ teaspoon salt

¼ teaspoon freshly ground black pepper

2 cups hot water

Cashew Cream (page 78), for garnish

¾ cup Lentil Almond Croutons (page 102), for garnish

1. Place 2 whole bell peppers, tomatoes, zucchini, avocado, carrot, lemon juice, sun-dried tomatoes, 3 tablespoons of hemp hearts, jalapeño, ginger, cumin, garlic, salt, and pepper into a high-speed blender.

2. Start blending while slowly adding the hot water. Blend until smooth and creamy. Taste and adjust seasoning to desired spiciness.

Continued ▶

3. Pour the soup into three bowls or jars and add a dollop of Cashew Cream to each. Garnish with diced red pepper, hemp seeds, and Lentil Almond Croutons.

PREP TIP: Make sure your garnishes are prepared for when your soup is ready. The soup itself only takes a few minutes to prep and blend. The garnishes, depending on what they are, may take a bit longer. I recommend the Lentil Almond Croutons for a crunch and basil for a fresh element.

VARIATION TIP: Always garnish your soup. Especially the creamy soups! Garnishes can look like fresh veggies and herbs such as diced red pepper, basil leaves, or dehydrated veggies like dried tomato slices or Caramelized Onions (page 128). Hemp seeds add a healthy dose of fat and protein. A dollop of Cashew Cream adds creaminess and extra fat. Kimchi and sauerkraut also make tasty gut-healing garnishes.

Per serving: Calories: 456; Total fat: 30g; Sodium: 61mg; Carbohydrates: 41g; Fiber: 14g; Sugar: 8g; Protein: 16g

RAW MEXI CHILI

PREP TIME: 10 minutes | YIELD: 2 or 3 servings (makes 5 cups)

Spice it up with this hearty, satisfying, and rich bowl of delicious chili. A great dish to serve to your family on a cool winter's eve or enjoy in front of the TV on game day! Tomatoes are loaded with vitamins A, C, and K, to name a few, and they are also high in the antioxidant lycopene. Needless to say, this simple and satisfying chili recipe will leave you happier and healthier.

Suggested Equipment: **Food processor or Blender**

½ cup sun-dried tomatoes, soaked 30 to 60 minutes, until tender

3 large juicy tomatoes, chopped

1 cup cherry tomatoes, sliced, divided

¼ sweet onion, chopped

1 cup fresh cilantro

1 garlic clove, minced

1 tablespoon minced jalapeño pepper

Juice of 1 lime

1 tablespoon chili powder

1 teaspoon cumin

¼ teaspoon Himalayan pink salt

Freshly ground black pepper

1 medium zucchini, diced into small cubes

1 red bell pepper, diced

1 stalk celery, chopped

½ cup corn kernels, fresh or frozen

1 avocado, sliced, for garnish

Cashew Sour Cream (page 113), for garnish

1. Combine sun-dried tomatoes, chopped tomatoes, ½ cup cherry tomatoes, onion, cilantro, garlic, jalapeño pepper, lime juice, chili powder, cumin, salt, and pepper in the food processor or blender and process into a thick paste.

2. Transfer to a bowl and fold in the zucchini, red pepper, celery, corn, and remaining ½ cup cherry tomatoes.

3. Garnish with fresh avocado slices, a dollop of Cashew Sour Cream, and freshly ground black pepper.

INGREDIENT TIP: For a heartier texture and more substance, add sprouted lentils to the dish.

Per serving: Calories: 377; Total fat: 17g; Sodium: 553mg; Carbohydrates: 57g; Fiber: 18g; Sugar: 23g; Protein: 12g

WATERMELON GAZPACHO

PREP TIME: 30 minutes | YIELD: 2 servings

Originating in Spain, this raw vegetable soup is usually served cold as an appetizer in the hot summer months. It is a light, refreshing summertime soup that is quick and easy to make and can be adjusted to your liking.

Suggested Equipment: **Food processor**

4 cups coarsely chopped seedless watermelon, divided

1 cucumber, peeled and diced, divided

3 Roma tomatoes, diced, divided

1 red bell pepper, diced, divided

¼ cup finely chopped fresh basil

¼ cup diced sweet onion

1 garlic clove, minced

2 tablespoons olive oil

2 tablespoons fresh lime or lemon juice

1 tablespoon balsamic or apple cider vinegar

½ cup soaked cashews or macadamia nuts (optional, see Tip)

2 tablespoons minced jalapeño pepper, (optional, see Tip)

Pinch Himalayan pink salt

Freshly ground black pepper

1 avocado, sliced, for garnish

Watermelon wedges, for garnish

Sprouted legumes, small handful, for garnish

1. In the food processor, combine 2 cups of the watermelon, half of the cucumber, 2 tomatoes, half of the bell pepper, the basil, onion, garlic, olive oil, lime juice, vinegar, soaked nuts and/or jalapeño (if using), salt, and pepper and process until blended but still chunky.

2. Pour the soup into a bowl and mix with the remaining watermelon, cucumber, tomato, and bell pepper. Cover the bowl and place in the refrigerator for 2 hours to chill.

3. To serve, divide between 2 bowls and garnish each bowl with half the avocado, a watermelon wedge, and sprouted legumes.

VARIATION TIP: You can add or replace many ingredients. Blending zucchini will give it a thicker texture. Sliced celery will add a crunch. Jalapeño pepper will give it a kick, and soaked macadamia or cashew nuts will add creaminess. You can leave out the watermelon and substitute fresh juicy peaches, or use an equivalent amount of tomatoes for a classic gazpacho. Play around with the ingredients and seasoning to make it your own!

PREP TIP: The soup can also be made in a high-speed blender. You can blend all ingredients for a smooth creamy soup, or leave some out for a chunkier soup.

Per serving, with garnishes (avocado, watermelon, sprouted legumes): Calories: 689; Total fat: 38g; Sodium: 33mg; Carbohydrates: 87g; Fiber: 15g; Sugar: 50g; Protein: 15g

HEALING ENERGY SOUP

PREP TIME: 5 minutes | YIELD: 2 servings

This healing recipe was inspired by Dr. Ann Wigmore, a world-renowned holistic health practitioner and raw food advocate. She would serve a bland blended green soup to her patients and students daily to provide optimal nutritional cleansing and healing. It was not glamorous, but it sure was nutritious! I've taken her nutritious concept and made it delicious in this healing energy soup!

Suggested Equipment: **High-speed blender**

2 cups baby kale

2 cups spinach

2 cups water

1 avocado

1 apple

Juice of 1 orange

Juice of 1 lime

½ cup broccoli sprouts

½ cup sprouted lentils

¼ cup hemp seeds

½-inch piece grated peeled ginger

1 tablespoon miso or coconut aminos

1 teaspoon spirulina or chlorella

Blend ingredients in a high-speed blender until smooth and creamy.

SERVING TIP: For a warm soup, use warm water or blend for 4 minutes to heat.

VARIATION TIP: Feel free to increase the nutritional value even more by adding superfoods like soaked goji berries, maca, or chia seeds. Garnish with your favorite toppings, such as orange wedges, sauerkraut, or sprouted chickpeas.

Per serving: Calories: 439; Total fat: 23g; Sodium: 458mg; Carbohydrates: 50g; Fiber: 17g; Sugar: 18g; Protein: 16g

KALE CAESAR SALAD

This Caesar salad dressing is an all-time crowd-pleaser. It's creamy and delicious and can be used as a dip for fresh veggies or as a spread for wraps. The dressing can be refrigerated for a week or frozen and used for future salads.

Suggested Equipment: **Dehydrator, High-speed blender**

For the dressing

¾ cup macadamia nuts or cashews, soaked (or Cashew Cream, page 78)

¼ cup pine nuts

3 soaked dates

5 basil leaves

4 tablespoons freshly squeezed lemon juice

3 tablespoons hemp seeds

1 teaspoon nutritional yeast

3 garlic cloves

¼ teaspoon Himalayan pink salt

¼ teaspoon freshly ground black pepper

¼ cup water

For the salad

3 cups kale, stemmed

2 cups chopped romaine lettuce

1 cup cherry tomatoes, halved

1 cup sprouts

¼ cup Coconut Bacon (page 101)

½ cup Lentil Almond Croutons (page 102)

To make the dressing

Blend all dressing ingredients in a high-speed blender until smooth and set aside, or refrigerate if using at a later date.

Continued ▶

To make the salad

1. In a large bowl, toss the kale and romaine lettuce with the dressing. Add the cherry tomatoes.

2. Divide the salad into 2 serving bowls. Top each bowl with fresh sprouts, Coconut Bacon, and Lentil Almond Croutons.

VARIATION TIP: If you don't have a dehydrator to make bacon and croutons, top this salad with Almond Rawmesan Cheese (page 141) and Seasoned Sprouted Chickpeas (page 106).

SUBSTITUTION TIP: Use soaked cashews in place of macadamia nuts.

Per serving: Calories: 961; Total fat: 80g; Sodium: 159mg; Carbohydrates: 57g; Fiber: 19g; Sugar: 21g; Protein: 24g

COCONUT BACON

If you ever have a craving for bacon but don't want the real thing, coconut bacon is the answer! Savory and crispy, it's a great addition to salads or even a vegan BLT sandwich. The secret ingredient: liquid smoke, which can be found at most grocery stores or online.

Suggested Equipment: **Dehydrator**

1 cup large unsweetened coconut flakes

1 tablespoon maple syrup

1 tablespoon coconut aminos or tamari

1 tablespoon extra-virgin olive oil

1 teaspoon liquid smoke

¼ teaspoon Himalayan pink salt

Pinch chili powder

Pinch smoked paprika

1. Toss all ingredients together in a mixing bowl.

2. Spread on a nonstick dehydrator sheet or parchment paper and dehydrate at 118°F for 4 hours.

3. Remove nonstick sheet and continue dehydrating for 4 more hours, or until crispy.

4. Store in a glass jar in the refrigerator.

VARIATION TIP: Try this recipe with thinly sliced zucchini or eggplant for an alternative.

Per serving (¼ cup): Calories: 147; Total fat: 14g; Sodium: 90mg; Carbohydrates: 8g; Fiber: 2g; Sugar: 4g; Protein: 1g

LENTIL ALMOND CROUTONS

PREP TIME: 20 minutes; plus dehydrating time
YIELD: 40 croutons (about 2 cups)

Besides the dehydrating time, these Lentil Almond Croutons are extremely fast to prepare. I love recipes that simply consist of adding all ingredients to a food processor and you're done! Spread, score, dehydrate, and you're left with crunchy, tasty nuggets to add to salads and soups. It's a great way to add crunch to your meal, and it's also a great source of protein!

Suggested Equipment: **Dehydrator, Food processor**

1 tablespoon ground flaxseed

1 tablespoon olive oil

2 tablespoons water

¾ cup sprouted lentils

½ cup almonds, soaked

¼ cup almond flour or almond meal

¼ cup sprouted buckwheat groats

1 teaspoon garlic powder

1 teaspoon onion powder

1 teaspoon dried oregano

1 teaspoon cumin

½ teaspoon thyme

¼ teaspoon Himalayan pink salt

1. In a small bowl, combine flaxseed, oil, and water and let sit for 5 minutes. Stir occasionally until mixture has thickened.

2. Process all ingredients, including the flaxseed mixture, until well combined. Spread a ½-inch layer of the mixture on nonstick dehydrator sheets or parchment paper and dehydrate at 118°F for 6 hours. Flip, remove the sheet of paper, and continue to dehydrate for 4 more hours, or until dry.

SUBSTITUTION TIP: Leave out the buckwheat if you don't have any sprouted. You can also use any sprouted legume. Leave out legumes altogether and use 1 cup almonds if you prefer.

INGREDIENT TIP: For the almond flour or meal, use the leftover pulp from making almond milk. For a salty, cheesy flavor, sprinkle Almond Rawmesan Cheese (page 141) on the croutons before dehydrating.

Per serving (½ cup): Calories: 239; Total fat: 17g; Sodium: 4mg; Carbohydrates: 18g; Fiber: 5g; Sugar: 1g; Protein: 9g

WALDORF SALAD

PREP TIME: 5 minutes | YIELD: 2 servings

The Waldorf salad is said to have been created by Oscar Tschirky, a maître d' of the Waldorf-Astoria Hotel in New York City. The recipe appeared in his comprehensive 1896 cookbook. It's traditionally made with a mayonnaise and whipped cream dressing, but a cashew and pine nut–based dressing makes for a delicious and creamy alternative. Crunchy walnuts and celery paired with sweet apples and grapes will make this salad continue to go down in history.

4 cups of chopped romaine lettuce

2 celery stalks, sliced

3 dates, chopped

1 whole apple, chopped

1 cup grapes, halved

½ cup walnuts, chopped

¼ cup parsley, chopped

4 tablespoons Kale Caesar Salad dressing (page 99)

Combine all salad ingredients. Toss with dressing right before serving.

VARIATION TIP: This salad also makes a good filling for lettuce wraps. Simply fill Bibb lettuce or romaine lettuce leaves with the salad mix and serve.

Per serving: Calories: 390; Total fat: 28g; Sodium: 253mg; Carbohydrates: 35g; Fiber: 8g; Sugar: 30g; Protein: 8g

CAULIFLOWER TABOULI SALAD

PREP TIME: 10 minutes | YIELD: 2 servings (4 cups)

This is a traditional Lebanese salad that typically uses bulgur wheat. Substituting cauliflower rice makes this a low-carb, grain-free, and gluten-free recipe. Parsley is extremely rich in nutrients including vitamin C, vitamin K, vitamin A, beta-carotene, folate, and iron. This salad can be enjoyed with a traditional olive oil and lemon juice dressing or the Mediterranean dressing from the Mediterranean Buddha Bowl recipe (page 106).

Suggested Equipment: **Food processor**

For the salad

½ cup cherry tomatoes finely chopped

1 cup cucumber, finely chopped

¼ teaspoon salt

2½ cups cauliflower

½ cup parsley, finely chopped

⅓ cup fresh mint, finely chopped

2 scallions, green and white parts, finely chopped

2 tablespoons hemp seeds

For the dressing

⅓ cup olive oil

3 to 4 tablespoons freshly squeezed lemon juice

1 garlic clove, minced or pressed

¼ teaspoon salt

Freshly ground black pepper

To make the salad

1. Combine chopped tomatoes and cucumber in a bowl and add ¼ teaspoon of salt. Mix to combine and let sit.

2. Pulse the cauliflower in the food processor until it reaches a rice-like texture. Transfer to another bowl.

3. Add the parsley and mint to the cauliflower.

4. Strain the water from the tomato and cucumber mixture, and add the mixture to the cauliflower.

5. Fold in the scallions and hemp seeds.

In a small bowl, whisk together all the dressing ingredients. Taste and adjust as needed. Add more lemon juice for a zing or more salt for overall flavor. Pour the dressing onto the salad and toss to combine.

EQUIPMENT TIP: If you don't have a food processor, you can use a grater to grate the cauliflower or a chef's knife to finely chop the cauliflower.

VARIATION TIP: You can use sprouted quinoa instead of cauliflower for a heartier and more filling salad.

Per serving: Calories: 427; Total fat: 40g; Sodium: 43mg; Carbohydrates: 13g; Fiber: 5g; Sugar: 5g; Protein: 7g

MEDITERRANEAN BUDDHA BOWL WITH SEASONED SPROUTED CHICKPEAS

PREP TIME: 15 minutes | **YIELD:** 2 servings

The Mediterranean lifestyle is one of the healthiest ways of eating, full of healthy fats and fresh vegetables. I lived on fresh, flavorful Greek salads when I was in Greece. One of the reasons their salads were so flavorful is because they keep their tomatoes on the counter or in the garden instead of the refrigerator. The flavor of tomatoes is killed by cold storage. If you have a green thumb, start growing your own! There is nothing more satisfying than a freshly picked tomato.

Suggested Equipment: **High-speed blender**

For the dressing

¾ cup olive oil

¼ cup tahini

¼ cup freshly squeezed lemon juice

1 teaspoon maple syrup

1 teaspoon dried oregano

1 garlic clove or 1 teaspoon, pressed or minced

Pinch Himalayan pink salt

Freshly ground black pepper

2 teaspoons Dijon mustard

For the chickpeas

2 cups sprouted chickpeas (see page 20)

2 tablespoons olive oil

2 teaspoons chili powder

2 teaspoons cumin

1 teaspoon oregano

1 teaspoon garlic powder

1 teaspoon onion powder

Freshly ground black pepper

¼ teaspoon turmeric

½ teaspoon Himalayan pink salt

For the salad

4 cups spinach or mixed greens

1 red bell pepper, chopped

½ cucumber, chopped into bite-size pieces

½ cup cherry tomatoes, whole

¼ cup kalamata olives

½ cup parsley, chopped

¼ cup sunflower seeds

¼ cup red onion, chopped

¼ cup Zucchini Hummus (page 150)

1 cup alfalfa sprouts, for garnish

½ cup Mediterranean dressing

1. To prepare the dressing, blend all the ingredients in a high-speed blender and process until well combined. Set aside.

2. To prepare the chickpeas, place sprouted chickpeas in a bowl, add the oil, spices, and salt to the chickpeas, and toss to coat. You can enjoy the chickpeas fresh or dehydrate them at 118°F for 4 to 6 hours or longer, depending on how dry you want them.

3. To prepare the salad, divide the spinach, bell pepper, cucumber, tomatoes, olives, parsley, sunflower seeds, red onion, and hummus between two bowls. Top with alfalfa sprouts, chickpeas, and dressing.

VARIATION TIP: Make this salad in jars for grab-and-go lunches! Start with the dressing on the bottom (or keep it separate). Then cherry tomatoes, bell peppers, cucumber, olives, chickpeas, sunflower seeds, spinach, and sprouts. If you do make salad jars, use whole cherry tomatoes. This will keep it as fresh as possible.

INGREDIENT TIP: Use as many or as few ingredients as you like. If you don't have olives or parsley, don't worry about it!

Per serving: Calories: 640; Total fat: 54g; Sodium: 432mg; Carbohydrates: 37g; Fiber: 15g; Sugar: 7g; Protein: 13g

SUMMER CITRUS SALAD

PREP TIME: 5 minutes | YIELD: 1 serving

A fresh, sweet and tangy explosion of citrus flavors including grapefruit, orange, kiwi, strawberries, and blueberries is served on a bed of spinach and topped with fresh mint leaves. This super simple fruit salad is packed with nutrients, making it ideal for lunch, supper, or even breakfast!

1 cup spinach

1 cup Citrus Fruit Salad (page 75)

1 tablespoon olive oil

1 tablespoon sunflower seeds

Mint leaves

1. Place spinach in a bowl and arrange fruit salad on top. Drizzle with olive oil and top with sunflower seeds.

2. Garnish with fresh mint leaves.

VARIATION TIP: Dress this salad with any dressing you like best. Orange Ginger (page 109), Mediterranean (page 106), or Berry Vinaigrette (page 114) will all work well with this salad.

Per serving: Calories: 324; Total fat: 19g; Sodium: 29mg; Carbohydrates: 41g; Fiber: 9g; Sugar: 26g; Protein: 4g

SUPER SEED POWER BOWL WITH ORANGE GINGER DRESSING

PREP TIME: 10 minutes | YIELD: 2 servings

It's all about the dressing! This is by far my favorite dressing, and it goes well with any salad. I find dressings are best made in a bullet blender if you have one. This salad can be made into a salad jar for a grab-and-go lunch. When eating a lot of raw veggies, make sure to chew your food really well to aid in digestion.

Suggested Equipment: **High-speed blender**

For the bowl

2 cups spinach

2 cups arugula or baby kale

1 carrot, spiralized or shredded

1 beet, spiralized or shredded

1 apple, shredded

1 cup snap peas, trimmed

1 avocado, sliced or cubed

½ yellow zucchini, sliced in half-moons

½ cup sprouted quinoa (see page 20)

2 tablespoons hemp seeds

2 tablespoons pumpkin seeds

2 tablespoons sunflower seeds

For the dressing

½ cup freshly squeezed orange juice

¼ cup tahini

1 tablespoon freshly squeezed lime juice

1 tablespoon apple cider vinegar

1 tablespoon grated peeled fresh ginger

1 tablespoon olive oil

1 teaspoon minced garlic

Pinch Himalayan pink salt

Continued ▶

To make the bowl

1. Divide the spinach and arugula evenly between two large serving bowls.

2. Add in distinct sections the carrot, beet, apple, snap peas, avocado, and zucchini.

3. Top each bowl with half of the quinoa, hemp seeds, pumpkin seeds, and sunflower seeds.

To make the dressing

Blend all the dressing ingredients in a high-speed blender. Add 2 to 3 tablespoons of the dressing to the salad right before eating.

VARIATION TIP: Make salad jars instead of bowls if you want to save for a later day or bring for lunches. Salad jars keep the veggies separated and ensure maximum freshness. Add the dressing to the bottom of the jar and then layer the sprouted quinoa, beets, carrots, apple, zucchini, snap peas, and seeds and top with leafy greens. Add fresh avocado right before eating.

Per serving: Calories: 544; Total fat: 36g; Sodium: 209mg; Carbohydrates: 51g; Fiber: 17g; Sugar: 17g; Protein: 18g

SPICY WALNUT PÂTÉ LETTUCE WRAPS

PREP TIME: 5 minutes | **YIELD:** 2 servings

Lettuce wraps and pâté are both staples in the raw, vegan diet, so it only makes sense to put them together—a quick, raw vegan lunch that tastes great and will satisfy your hunger. Walnuts are an excellent source of heart-healthy omega-3 fatty acids, which are also healthy for the brain.

2 romaine lettuce leaves   **1 cup Spicy Walnut Pâté (page 151)**

Stuff lettuce leaves with pâté, wrap, and enjoy!

VARIATION TIP: You can layer the lettuce wraps with Dill Cashew Cream Cheese (page 88) or Caesar salad dressing (page 99) first, then add the pâté, and top with fresh alfalfa sprouts.

Per serving: Calories: 137; Total fat: 11g; Sodium: 132mg; Carbohydrates: 8g; Fiber: 3g; Sugar: 2g; Protein: 3g

LENTIL WALNUT TACO SALAD

PREP TIME: 15 minutes | **YIELD:** 4 servings

This walnut lentil taco meat is a perfect alternative to meat with a spicy Mexican flair. Full of fiber, healthy omega-3 fatty acids, and protein, this is a versatile dish that can be made into taco lettuce wraps or a taco salad.

Suggested Equipment: **Food processor**

For the taco filling

1 cup walnuts

1 cup sprouted lentils (see page 20)

1 tablespoon olive oil

2 teaspoons chili powder

2 teaspoons cumin

2 teaspoons oregano

½ teaspoon garlic powder

¼ teaspoon Himalayan pink salt

Freshly Ground Black Pepper

For the salad

6 cups romaine lettuce, chopped

1 red bell pepper, chopped

1 Roma tomato, diced

1 avocado, sliced or chopped

½ cup corn kernels

¼ cup red onion, finely chopped

¼ cup cilantro, finely chopped

Mango Salsa (page 148), Guacamole (page 149), and Cashew Sour Cream (page 113), for toppings

1. To make the taco filling, process taco ingredients in a food processor until well combined and the texture of ground beef. Adjust spices to taste.

2. To make the salad, divide romaine, bell pepper, tomato, avocado, and corn between 4 bowls. Top with ¼ cup taco mixture, red onion, cilantro, and your desired toppings such as Mango Salsa (page 148), Guacamole (page 149), and Cashew Sour Cream (page 113).

VARIATION TIP: You can substitute any sprouted legume for the lentils or leave them out completely and add more walnuts.

PREP TIP: Another way to prepare the taco "meat" is to crumble it up on a dehydrator tray and dehydrate it at 115°F for 2 hours, until dry on the outside and still soft on the inside.

Per serving: Calories: 379; Total fat: 31g; Sodium: 36mg; Carbohydrates: 25g; Fiber: 9g; Sugar: 5g; Protein: 11g

CASHEW SOUR CREAM

PREP TIME: 5 minutes, plus soaking time | YIELD: 1 cup

What would cream lovers do without cashews? Cashews are spectacular little gems when it comes to dairy-free living. Providing a rich and creamy texture, as well as a slight sweetness with a little tang, this cashew sour cream is a perfect complement to spicy meals. Try it with Raw Mexi Chili (page 95) or Lentil Walnut Taco Salad (page 112).

Suggested Equipment: **High-speed blender**

1 cup cashews, soaked overnight and drained

¼ cup water

1 tablespoon freshly squeezed lemon juice

1 tablespoon apple cider vinegar

Pinch Himalayan pink salt

1. Blend ingredients in a high-speed blender until smooth and creamy.

2. Store in a glass container in the refrigerator.

VARIATION TIP: To make this recipe rich in probiotics and good for the gut, add a probiotic capsule to the cream and let it sit overnight to ferment. The fermentation will create a tangy flavor, but the lemon juice and vinegar will balance it with sour flavor.

Per serving (¼ cup): Calories: 197; Total fat: 16g; Sodium: 6mg; Carbohydrates: 11g; Fiber: 1g; Sugar: 2g; Protein: 5g

RAINBOW SALAD IN A JAR WITH BERRY VINAIGRETTE

This is a salad for the kiddos! Kids love playing with the colors of the rainbow, so if you're making this salad for them, place the veggies on a plate in the shape of a rainbow instead of a jar. The berry vinaigrette is a deliciously sweet and tangy addition full of fiber and antioxidants.

Suggested Equipment: **High-speed blender**

For the vinaigrette

- ½ heaping cup berries, fresh or frozen
- ⅓ cup olive oil
- 2 tablespoons balsamic vinegar
- 2 tablespoons water
- 1 teaspoon maple syrup
- ½ teaspoon minced garlic
- ½ teaspoon minced peeled ginger
- Pinch Himalayan pink salt
- Freshly ground black pepper

For the salad

- 1 red bell pepper, chopped
- 1 carrot, shredded
- 1 yellow bell pepper, chopped
- 1 beet, shredded
- ½ cup blueberries
- ½ cup blackberries
- 4 cups spinach
- 4 tablespoons hemp seeds
- 4 tablespoons sunflower seeds

1. Blend vinaigrette ingredients in a high-speed blender until smooth.

2. Add ¼ cup of the vinaigrette to the bottom of the jar. Layer vegetables on top of the dressing, making spinach the last layer, and top with hemp and sunflower seeds.

3. Store in the refrigerator for up to 5 days.

VARIATION TIP: If you keep the salad dressing separate, feel free to layer the vegetables in the colors of the rainbow.

Per serving: Calories: 392; Total fat: 24g; Sodium: 112mg; Carbohydrates: 36g; Fiber: 12g; Sugar: 13g; Protein: 14g

Rainbow Pad Thai
with Spicy Almond Sauce,
page 118

7 ENTICING ENTRÉES

RAINBOW PAD THAI WITH SPICY ALMOND SAUCE

PREP TIME: 25 minutes | YIELD: 2 to 4 servings

This would make a perfect weeknight meal when you want something satisfying and healthy on the table fast. After making it the first time, I guarantee you that it will be a staple in your house as it is in mine. Colorful and full of flavor, it's a great introduction to a raw food diet. The ginger and garlic support immunity, circulation, and digestion and the rainbow of colors adds antioxidants in the form of phytonutrients!

Suggested Equipment: **High-speed blender, Mandoline, Spiralizer, or Vegetable peeler**

For the the almond sauce

½ cup raw almond butter

4 tablespoons water

3 tablespoons lime juice

3 tablespoons olive oil

2 tablespoons, coconut aminos

1 tablespoon ginger, peeled and grated

1 tablespoon jalapeño pepper, minced

1 teaspoon garlic, minced

1 teaspoon maple syrup

1 teaspoon apple cider vinegar

Pinch cayenne pepper

Pinch salt

For the salad

1 medium zucchini, spiralized, julienned on a mandoline, or shaved with a peeler

2 carrots, shaved or julienned

3 scallions, white and green parts, chopped, divided

1 red bell pepper, julienned

1 orange bell pepper, julienned

3 cups kale, stemmed, chiffonade into very thin strips

1 teaspoon olive or sesame oil

1 cup purple cabbage, cut very thin (optional)

1 cup kelp noodles, rinsed and cut into sections with scissors (optional)

2 tablespoons hemp seeds

Almonds or peanuts, chopped, for garnish

Sesame seeds, for garnish

½ cup chopped cilantro, for garnish

3 tablespoons dressing per serving

1. To make the almond sauce, place all the ingredients into a high-speed blender and blend until smooth.

2. To make the salad, in a large mixing bowl, combine the zucchini, carrots, two-thirds of the scallions, and the bell peppers.

3. Massage the kale with oil to soften it. Add it to the bowl.

4. If using, add the cabbage and kelp noodles to the bowl.

5. Divide the salad ingredients into two to four bowls and add 3 tablespoons of sauce to each bowl. Mix well. Top with hemp seeds. Garnish the salads with chopped almonds or peanuts, the remaining scallions, sesame seeds, and cilantro. If you want it warmed, place each plate in the dehydrator until warm.

INGREDIENT TIP: When looking for nut butters, make sure to check out the ingredient list. You want to look for the word raw in the name or at least just one word in the ingredient list, such as peanuts or almonds. Do not choose a variety that has been roasted or that has any additional ingredients like sugar or oil.

VARIATION TIP: There are a lot of different colorful vegetables you can add or swap out. You can add mushrooms if you like, for instance. If you don't have sesame oil, olive oil will work. If you don't have almond butter, raw peanut butter will also work.

Per serving: Calories: 388; Total fat: 24g; Sodium: 323mg; Carbohydrates: 36g; Fiber: 13g; Sugar: 12g; Protein: 13g

COLLARD WRAPS

PREP TIME: 15 minutes | YIELD: 2 servings

These wraps are surprisingly easy to make, especially if you have the almond sauce ready-made. Collard leaves make perfect wraps for the raw vegan diet. Spread your favorite vegan cheese, veggie pâté, or nut butter sauce, load it up with your favorite veggies, roll and you're ready to go! The spicy almond sauce is the same sauce used in the Rainbow Pad Thai (page 118) so if you made it for that recipe, you should have enough left over for this recipe.

Suggested Equipment: **High-speed blender**

2 large collard leaves	**¾ cup lentil sprouts (see page 20)**
½ cup Spicy Almond Sauce (page 118)	**½ cup chopped cilantro**
1 large carrot, shredded	**1 avocado, sliced**
1 cucumber, julienned into 3-inch strips	**1 cup alfalfa sprouts**

1. Place the collard leaves on a cutting board, shiny-side down. Cut the leaves in half down the spine so you have 4 halves.

2. Spread 2 tablespoons of almond sauce on each half leaf.

3. Divide the ingredients between the leaves in this order: carrot, cucumber, lentil sprouts, cilantro, avocado, and alfalfa.

4. Roll leaves tight and serve.

VARIATION TIP: These wraps will also work well with the Kale Caesar Salad dressing (page 99). Layer the collard wraps with Caesar salad dressing and veggies, then dip in the almond sauce. Collard leaves can also be used to make wraps with the filling from Lentil Walnut Taco Salad (page 112) and all its fixings.

Per serving: Calories: 409; Total fat: 30g; Sodium: 266mg; Carbohydrates: 32g; Fiber: 12g; Sugar: 7g; Protein: 10g

FETTUCCINE ALFREDO

PREP TIME: 30 minutes | YIELD: 2 servings

This is a delicious and healthy spin on traditional fettuccine Alfredo. The sauce tastes decadent yet is superlight and energizing thanks to the cauliflower base. Paired with the rich and savory Sunflower Seedballs (page 122), the zucchini pasta won't weigh you down either.

Suggested Equipment: **High-speed blender, Veggie spiralizer**

For the pasta

3 zucchini

Pinch Himalayan pink salt

For the sauce

1 small head of cauliflower, chopped (about 2 cups)

2 garlic cloves, pressed or minced

½ cup water

¼ cup full-fat coconut cream

1 tablespoon olive oil

2 teaspoons lemon juice

¼ teaspoon Himalayan pink salt

Freshly ground black pepper to taste

1 tablespoon nutritional yeast

Almond Rawmesan Cheese (page 141), for garnish

Sunflower Seedballs, for garnish

To make the pasta

Spiralize zucchini with a spiralizer, mandoline, or vegetable peeler and toss with a pinch of salt to soften. Set aside.

To make the alfredo sauce

1. Blend Alfredo sauce ingredients in a high-speed blender.

2. Drain any water that may have released from the zucchini and pat dry. Add Alfredo sauce to zucchini pasta.

3. Garnish with almond cheese and serve with Sunflower Seedballs.

VARIATION TIP: You can use any raw noodles such as raw kelp noodles or spiralized butternut squash.

Per serving (without Sunflower Seedballs): Calories: 197; Total fat: 14g; Sodium: 68mg; Carbohydrates: 17g; Fiber: 6g; Sugar: 7g; Protein: 6g

SUNFLOWER SEEDBALLS

PREP TIME: 10 minutes | YIELD: 8 or 9 balls

These delicious, savory balls are the raw vegan version of meatballs! Quick and easy to make, these little gems are full of omega-3 fatty acids, vitamin E, fiber, and protein. Whether you serve them warm on a pasta dish with tomato sauce or eat them cold as a great grab-and-go snack, rest assured your blood sugar will remain low and your energy levels high.

Suggested Equipment: **High-speed blender, Small ice cream scoop or melon baller, if available**

¾ cup raw, unsalted sunflower seeds

½ cup walnuts

3 tablespoons flaxseed, ground

¼ cup sweet onion, finely chopped

¼ cup orange or red bell pepper, finely chopped

¼ cup celery, finely chopped

1 tablespoon coconut aminos or soy sauce

1 teaspoon Italian herbs, or basil, or oregano

2 teaspoons water, if needed

1. Grind the sunflower seeds, walnuts, and flaxseed separately in a high-speed blender or coffee grinder. Transfer to a mixing bowl.

2. Add the onion, bell pepper, and celery to the bowl.

3. Add the coconut aminos and herbs and mix well. The dough will be sticky; if not, add water by the teaspoon and mix.

4. Form into 1-inch balls using a small ice cream scoop and put on a nonstick cookie tray or use parchment paper. If you do not have an ice cream scoop, a spoon works just fine.

5. Place in dehydrator at 118°F to warm for 30 minutes. You can also serve the seedballs cold as soon as they are made. They go great with kelp noodle pasta and raw tomato sauce.

6. Store in an airtight glass container in refrigerator or freezer.

PREP TIP: To save even more time, throw your veggies into a food processor and pulse a few times to finely chop. Doubling the recipe is a good idea as these little balls freeze very well. I suggest wrapping each individually with cling wrap and then storing in an airtight glass container in the freezer.

EQUIPMENT TIP: I find the coffee grinder works faster and better than the blender for grinding nuts and seeds, but either will work just fine.

Per serving: Calories: 138; Total fat: 12g; Sodium: 46mg; Carbohydrates: 6g; Fiber: 3g; Sugar: 1g; Protein: 4g

LENTIL WALNUT TACOS

PREP TIME: 5 minutes | YIELD: 2 servings

Tacos are a great option for the whole family. The Mango Salsa (page 148) adds a touch of sweetness and heat while the Cashew Sour Cream (page 113) cools with a tangy creaminess. The lentil walnut filling is a perfect meat alternative as it's full of healthy fats and protein. Once all four recipes are made, it only takes a few minutes to assemble into tacos.

Bibb lettuce or romaine lettuce leaves

¾ cup Lentil Walnut Taco Salad filling (page 112), divided

1 tomato, chopped

1 red bell pepper, thinly sliced

½ cup Guacamole (page 149)

½ cup Mango Salsa (page 148)

⅓ cup Cashew Sour Cream (page 113)

2 scallions, white and green parts, chopped

1. Stuff lettuce leaves with taco filling.

2. Top with tomato, bell pepper, Guacamole, Mango Salsa, Cashew Sour Cream, and scallions.

INGREDIENT TIP: You can dress the tacos with your favorite fixings. Add more spice to the taco meat if you want more of a kick. Serve in lettuce wraps, veggie wraps, or enjoy as a taco salad.

Per serving: Calories: 520; Total fat: 40g; Sodium: 28mg; Carbohydrates: 39g; Fiber: 14g; Sugar: 7g; Protein: 12g

CAULIFLOWER MASH WITH TAHINI MISO GRAVY AND CARAMELIZED ONIONS

What can't cauliflower do? Cauliflower is the best low-carb alternative to high-starch potato and high-glycemic white rice. I've even used it to replace the chicken in hot Buffalo wings and bulgur wheat in tabouli salad. To make this raw recipe as close to the creamy texture of mashed potato as possible, I used pine nuts and avocado.

Suggested Equipment: **Food processor**

1 small head cauliflower, chopped (about 3 cups)

¼ cup pine nuts

½ avocado

1 tablespoon miso or ¼ teaspoon Himalayan pink salt

1 garlic clove, pressed or minced

Freshly ground black pepper

¼ cup chopped parsley

Caramelized Onions (page 128), for garnish

Tahini Miso Gravy (page 127), for serving

1. Place cauliflower, pine nuts, avocado, miso, garlic, and pepper in the food processor. Process until your desired creamy consistency is reached.

2. Transfer to a bowl and mix in parsley. Top with Caramelized Onions or your garnish of choice, and serve with Tahini Miso Gravy.

INGREDIENT TIP: If you don't have avocado, use ¼ cup of full-fat coconut cream instead.

Per serving (without garnishes): Calories: 244; Total fat: 19g; Sodium: 323mg; Carbohydrates: 18g; Fiber: 8g; Sugar: 4g; Protein: 7g

TAHINI MISO GRAVY

PREP TIME: 5 minutes | **YIELD:** 1 cup

When the holidays come around, don't miss out on the gravy! This is a delicious and savory alternative to traditional gravy. Serve it on top of Cauliflower Mash (page 126) or as a dressing for the Dragon Bowl (page 129). Make sure to separate the gravy into two portions if you choose to thicken it, as the thinner version works best for the Dragon Bowl.

Suggested Equipment: **High-speed blender**

¼ cup tahini

2 tablespoons soy or chickpea miso

2 tablespoons coconut aminos

2 tablespoons coconut cream
  from a can of full-fat coconut milk

1 tablespoon nutritional yeast

1 garlic clove, minced or pressed

1 teaspoon maple syrup

1 cup water

2 teaspoons psyllium husk powder
  (optional)

1. Blend the tahini, miso, coconut aminos, coconut cream, yeast, garlic, maple syrup, and water in a high-speed blender until creamy.

2. Use the psyllium husk powder as a thickener. Leave it out for a thinner gravy or add more for a thicker gravy.

INGREDIENT TIP: Make sure to blend the psyllium husk powder and not stir as it will clump up.

Per serving (½ cup): Calories: 274; Total fat: 20g; Sodium: 1125mg; Carbohydrates: 17g; Fiber: 4g; Sugar: 3g; Protein: 8g

CARAMELIZED ONIONS

PREP TIME: 5 minutes, plus dehydrating time | YIELD: 1 cup

Sweet, pungent, and crispy describes these dehydrated onions. They make great garnishes for Cauliflower Mash (page 126), blended soups, and creamy pastas.

Suggested Equipment: **Dehydrator**

1 cup sweet onion, sliced

1 tablespoon maple syrup

1 tablespoon soy sauce
or coconut aminos

1 tablespoon miso

1. Thinly slice the onion and mix it with the maple syrup, soy sauce, and miso.

2. Let it marinate for 2 hours and then dehydrate at 115°F until sticky and dry. Leave it longer if you want it crispier.

INGREDIENT TIP: Since these onions are being eaten raw, make sure to choose a mature, sweet onion as opposed to a young onion, as otherwise it will be too strong and pungent to enjoy raw, no matter how much maple syrup you add. A younger onion will be smaller and more green.

Per serving (½ cup): Calories: 79; Total fat: <1g; Sodium: 443mg; Carbohydrates: 18g; Fiber: 1g; Sugar: 9g; Protein: 1g

DRAGON BOWL
WITH TAHINI MISO GRAVY

PREP TIME: 15 minutes, plus sprouting time | **YIELD:** 2 servings

This Asian-inspired nourishing bowl is similar in concept to the well-known Buddha bowls. Its uniqueness is derived from its sauce, the Tahini Miso Gravy (page 127). This thick, creamy, and nutritious sauce brings the same old veggies to life.

1 beet, shredded

2 carrots, shredded

½ cup fresh broccoli, radish, or alfalfa sprouts

½ cup wild rice or quinoa, sprouted (see page 20)

½ cup seasoned chickpeas, sprouted

½ cucumber, julienned

1 avocado, sliced

1 red bell pepper, sliced

2 tablespoons hemp seeds

½ cup Tahini Miso Gravy (page 127), divided

Mix all ingredients together (except gravy) and divide between two bowls. Dress with Tahini Miso Gravy.

VARIATION TIP: Add any fresh veggies you like, depending on what ingredients you have on hand. Try a shredded apple instead of a beet.

Per serving: Calories: 600; Total fat: 32g; Sodium: 650mg; Carbohydrates: 66g; Fiber: 17g; Sugar: 12g; Protein: 20g

RAW VEGAN MAC 'N' CHEESE

PREP TIME: 10 minutes | YIELD: 2 servings

This recipe is a classic family favorite, a comforting food that can be enjoyed individually too. It takes no time at all to prepare. Garnish with freshly ground black pepper and serve it with a side of raw ketchup for the kiddos. Although simple, this recipe packs a powerful punch of nutrients. Did you know that nutritional yeast is a complete protein? One tablespoon contains 2 grams of protein, B vitamins, and trace minerals.

Suggested Equipment: **High-speed blender, Spiralizer or Peeler**

For the Cashew Cheese Sauce

1½ cups cashews, soaked and drained

½ red bell pepper, chopped

¼ cup water, plus more if needed

¼ cup nutritional yeast

1½ tablespoons freshly squeezed lemon juice or apple cider vinegar

1 teaspoon onion powder

¾ teaspoon sea salt

½ teaspoon garlic powder

¼ teaspoon turmeric powder

For the noodles

3 zucchini or 4 cups raw kelp noodles, or a mixture of both

To make the Cashew Cheese Sauce

In a blender, combine cashews, bell pepper, ¼ cup water, yeast, lemon juice, onion powder, sea salt, garlic powder, and turmeric. If you are having trouble getting the mixture to blend properly, turn your high-speed blender off and scrape down the sides with a spatula. Then, continue blending, going from slow to high speed. If needed, add water, 1 tablespoon at a time, until the desired consistency has been reached. Don't add too much! You want this cheese sauce to be nice and thick.

1. Spiralize the zucchini. If you don't have a spiralizer, you can use a carrot peeler to create the zucchini noodles. To soften the zucchini noodles, sprinkle with salt and let sit for 10 minutes, and then rinse and pat dry. If you choose to go with kelp noodles, soak them in warm water to soften, then pat the noodles dry.

2. Add ¾ cup of the cheese sauce to the rinsed and dried noodles, tossing to coat.

PREP TIP: Soaking cashews in water for a minimum of 20 minutes to a maximum of overnight will make the blending process faster and easier. Salting the zucchini or soaking the kelp noodles before starting the cheese sauce ensures soft noodles when the sauce is ready.

EQUIPMENT TIP: If you don't have a high-speed blender, you can use your food processor on high. Just make sure the cashews have been presoaked, to ensure a smooth result.

Per serving: Calories: 367; Total fat: 25g; Sodium: 331mg; Carbohydrates: 30g; Fiber: 6g; Sugar: 8g; Protein: 15g

SPROUTED LENTIL STEW WITH SPANISH CAULIFLOWER RICE

PREP TIME: 40 minutes, plus sprouting time | **YIELD**: 4 servings

When the weather turns cold, I think of soups, stews, and warmth! Just because we are raw foodies, doesn't mean we have to eat everything cold. Place the bowls of stew in the dehydrator at 118°F for 30 minutes or until warm, and enjoy! Hearty, flavorful and nutritious, this stew pairs well with cauliflower rice. If the lentils are sprouted and the tomato sauce is prepared, this is a quick and easy recipe to make.

Suggested Equipment: **Food processor**

For the cauliflower rice

2 cups cauliflower, chopped

½ teaspoon cumin

¼ teaspoon Himalayan pink salt

¼ teaspoon onion powder

¼ teaspoon garlic powder

Freshly ground black pepper

For the stew

1 cup sprouted lentils (see page 20)

1 tomato, chopped

1 carrot, finely chopped

1 avocado, chopped

1 cup zucchini, chopped

½ cup celery, chopped

¼ teaspoon dried thyme

¼ teaspoon dried oregano

1 ¼ cups Sun-Dried Tomato Sauce (page 137)

Parsley, for garnish

1. To make the rice, in the food processor, pulse the cauliflower with cumin, salt, onion powder, garlic powder, and pepper until it reaches a rice-like consistency.

2. To make the stew, combine the lentils, tomato, carrot, avocado, zucchini, celery, thyme, oregano, and tomato sauce. Divide between 2 bowls, garnish with parsley, and serve with cauliflower rice.

3. Place in the dehydrator for 30 minutes to warm.

VARIATION TIP: Feel free to add more vegetables to the stew. Try serving it with sprouted wild rice instead of cauliflower rice for a heartier meal.

INGREDIENT TIP: I like to use green lentils when preparing stews as they tend to hold their form better than red lentils.

Per serving: Calories: 236; Total fat: 14g; Sodium: 173mg; Carbohydrates: 28g; Fiber: 9g; Sugar: 10g; Protein: 8g

JACKFRUIT SLOPPY JOES

PREP TIME: 15 minutes | YIELD: 2 to 4 servings

This recipe takes no time at all if the tomato sauce is prepared in advance and the bread has completed dehydrating. Then it's a quick blend and serve. Jackfruit is a great vegan substitution for meat. I have made jackfruit fish tacos, pulled pork, and sloppy joes!

Suggested Equipment: **High-speed blender**

1 (20-ounce) can jackfruit, in water or brine, or a fresh jackfruit, halved and cored, fruit removed

1 cup Sun-Dried Tomato Sauce (page 137)

½ small sweet onion, finely chopped

1 carrot, finely grated

1 tablespoon olive oil

1 tablespoon coconut aminos or soy sauce

1 tablespoon vegan Worcestershire sauce (optional)

2 teaspoons chili powder

1 teaspoon cumin

1 teaspoon garlic powder

1 teaspoon maple syrup

Freshly ground black pepper

4 Everything Bagel halves (page 86) or 4 pieces of Italian Onion Bread (page 135) or 4 Bibb or romaine lettuce leaves

1. Drain and rinse the canned jackfruit. Cut the triangular cores off and separate the jackfruit into strands. Transfer to a bowl.

2. Add the tomato sauce, onion, carrot, olive oil, coconut aminos, Worcestershire sauce (if using), chili powder, cumin, garlic powder, maple syrup, and pepper to a high-speed blender and blend until smooth. Add to the bowl of jackfruit, stirring to combine.

3. Serve the jackfruit mixture on top of Everything Bagels, Italian Onion Bread, or stuffed in lettuce wraps.

Per serving: Calories: 823; Total fat: 63g; Sodium: 656mg; Carbohydrates: 6g; Fiber: 26g; Sugar: 20g; Protein: 21g

ITALIAN ONION BREAD

PREP TIME: 20 minutes, plus soaking and dehydrating time | **YIELD:** 10 pieces of bread

What is life without bread? Actually, I haven't eaten bread in a long time and when I do have a craving, I whip up this soft and savory treat. Just because you're eating raw and vegan doesn't mean you have to quit eating all your favorite foods. Spread the bread batter as thick or as thin as you like on the dehydrator trays, but don't spread it too thin or the bread will become crackers.

Suggested Equipment: **Food processor, Dehydrator**

¾ **cup pecans, soaked**

¾ **cup sunflower seeds, soaked 8 hours or overnight**

1 sweet onion, chopped

1 celery stalk, finely chopped

½ **cup zucchini, chopped**

½ **cup flaxseed, soaked in ½ cup water, 8 hours or overnight**

½ **cup almond flour or oat flour**

¼ **cup psyllium husk powder**

¼ **cup hemp seeds**

1 tablespoon apple cider vinegar

1 tablespoon olive oil

2 teaspoons dried Italian herbs or rosemary

½ **teaspoon Himalayan pink salt**

1. Rinse the pecans and sunflower seeds well. Add them and the rest of the ingredients to a food processor and process until you get a smooth batter.

2. Spread the mixture into a square on a nonstick dehydrator sheet or parchment paper, and score into bread-size pieces. Dehydrate at 115°F for 4 hours, flip and peel off nonstick sheet or parchment, and dehydrate directly on the grates for another 6 to 8 hours or until dry.

3. Once dry, store in an airtight container in the refrigerator or freezer.

VARIATION TIP: Pecans can be replaced with walnuts, and the sunflower seeds with pumpkin seeds. The Italian herbs can be replaced with dried rosemary, the psyllium husk powder with ground flaxseed, and almond or oat flour with ground sprouted buckwheat.

Per serving (1 slice): Calories: 237; Total fat: 20g; Sodium: 7mg; Carbohydrates: 13g; Fiber: 9g; Sugar: 2g; Protein: 7g

RAW LASAGNA WITH BASIL PESTO AND BRAZIL NUT RICOTTA

PREP TIME: 45 minutes | **YIELD:** 2 servings

Meet the clean-eating version of your favorite comfort food: la la lasagna! Cheesy Brazil Nut Ricotta (page 139), herby pesto, and shaved zucchini noodles come together to make a delicious rich stack that won't weigh you down. Feel free to make it your own by adding olives, mushrooms, or sun-dried tomatoes.

Suggested Equipment: **Food processor, Mandoline**

2 zucchini

¼ teaspoon Himalayan pink salt

½ cup Basil Pesto (page 138)

½ cup Brazil Nut Ricotta (page 139)

½ cup Sun-Dried Tomato Sauce (page 137)

2 cups spinach, massaged with ¼ teaspoon olive oil

1 tomatoes, thinly sliced

1. Create the lasagna noodles by slicing the zucchini on a mandoline, or with a knife, into long, thin strips. Sprinkle the zucchini with the salt and let sit for 10 minutes to soften. Then rinse and pat dry.

2. On two plates, arrange some of the zucchini ribbons on the bottom, top with a layer of pesto, ricotta, tomato sauce, spinach, tomato, more zucchini ribbons, and so on until you have three layers of zucchini—bottom, middle, and top.

INGREDIENT TIP: Depending on what you have in the pantry, the ingredients can be switched up and still give you the same incredible taste. Try macadamia nuts instead of cashews in the tomato sauce, almonds instead of Brazil nuts in the ricotta cheese, and cilantro instead of basil in the pesto.

Per serving: Calories: 611; Total fat: 53g; Sodium: 767mg; Carbohydrates: 31g; Fiber: 10g; Sugar: 12g; Protein: 15g

SUN-DRIED TOMATO SAUCE

PREP TIME: 10 minutes, plus soaking time | YIELD: 2¼ cups

This sweet, creamy, and flavorful sauce can be used in any recipe requiring tomato sauce—chili, pizza, pasta, or lasagna, you name it. This recipe is thick, which is necessary for the Raw Lasagna with Basil Pesto and Brazil Nut Ricotta (page 136) and pizza, and can be thinned for pasta by adding a bit of the soaked date water.

Suggested Equipment: **High-speed blender**

4 large ripe tomatoes or 5 medium tomatoes, diced

½ cup sun-dried tomatoes, soaked in warm water for at least 30 minutes

½ cup cashews, soaked in warm water for 1 hour or overnight and drained

2 dates, soaked in warm water for at least 30 minutes and drained

2 tablespoons olive oil

2 teaspoons minced garlic

1 teaspoon dried oregano

1 teaspoon dried basil

¼ teaspoon Himalayan pink salt

Blend all of the ingredients in a high-speed blender until smooth.

VARIATION TIP: The soaked cashews add creaminess to this tomato sauce. They can be substituted with soaked macadamia nuts instead. The dates add sweetness, and can be substituted with maple syrup.

Per serving (¼ cup): Calories: 106; Total fat: 7g; Sodium: 137mg; Carbohydrates: 11g; Fiber: 2g; Sugar: 5g; Protein: 3g

BASIL PESTO

PREP TIME: 10 minutes | YIELD: 1 cup

Homemade basil pesto is an utter delight and really versatile. It's easy to make and freezes extremely well. Once prepared, toss it with zucchini noodles for a quick and easy dinner or spread it on crackers for a light and fresh dip.

Suggested Equipment: **Food processor**

1 cup packed basil or cilantro

1 cup packed baby spinach

½ cup walnuts

¼ cup pine nuts

½ cup zucchini, chopped

2 garlic cloves, minced

2 tablespoons olive oil

2 tablespoons lemon juice

½ teaspoon salt

Combine all the ingredients in a food processor and pulse until well mixed.

VARIATION TIP: Many ingredients can be substituted in this recipe. Try cilantro instead of basil, baby kale instead of spinach, pecans instead of walnuts, or apple cider vinegar instead of lemon juice.

Per serving (½ cup): Calories: 456; Total fat: 46g; Sodium: 606mg; Carbohydrates: 12g; Fiber: 5g; Sugar: 3g; Protein: 9g

BRAZIL NUT RICOTTA

This is a nutty and flavorful cheese that freezes well and is very versatile. Try it on homemade pizza, zucchini pasta, Caesar salad, as a dip for veggies, layered on raw crackers, or as a base for spinach dip. It's always nice to have some nut cheese on hand for those late-night cheesy cravings.

Suggested Equipment: **Food processor**

¾ cup Brazil nuts

¼ cup pine nuts

3 tablespoons lemon juice

1 tablespoon nutritional yeast

½ teaspoon garlic powder

Pinch Himalayan pink salt

Process all of the ingredients in a food processor until mixed and they achieve the texture of ricotta cheese.

VARIATION TIP: Almonds can be used instead of Brazil nuts.

Per serving (½ cup): Calories: 417; Total fat: 40g; Sodium: 7mg; Carbohydrates: 10g; Fiber: 4g; Sugar: 1g; Protein: 10g

CREAMY AVOCADO PESTO PASTA WITH ALMOND RAWMESAN CHEESE

PREP TIME: 15 minutes | YIELD: 2 servings

If you have the Almond Rawmesan Cheese (page 141) already made, this is a very quick recipe to make. Just blend, spiralize, and enjoy! Full of healthy fats from the avocado, olive oil and almonds, this dreamy creamy pesto pasta will leave you feeling full and that carb craving satisfied.

Suggested Equipment: **High-speed blender, Veggie spiralizer**

3 zucchini

¼ teaspoon Himalayan pink salt, plus a pinch

2 avocados

½ cup fresh basil, packed

1 tablespoon olive oil

1 tablespoon freshly squeezed lemon juice

1 garlic clove, minced

Almond Rawmesan Cheese (page 141)

Basil leaves, for garnish

1. To make the pasta, spiralize the zucchini and place in a bowl with salt to soften for 10 minutes. Then, rinse and pat the zucchini dry.

2. To make the sauce, place the avocados, basil, olive oil, lemon juice, garlic, and a pinch of salt in to a high-speed blender and blend until smooth and creamy.

3. Combine the avocado sauce with the pasta and top with almond cheese and basil leaves.

INGREDIENT TIP: You can garnish this pasta with whatever you like or have on hand. Try the Coconut Bacon (page 101) or Seasoned Sprouted Chickpeas (page 106). I like to add sauerkraut to everything to ensure easy digestion and good gut health.

VARIATION TIP: If you have leftover Sun-Dried Tomato Sauce (page 137), pour that on the spiralized zucchini noodles for a different flavor. Don't forget to garnish!

Per serving (without Almond Rawmesan Cheese): Calories: 402; Total fat: 34g; Sodium: 337mg; Carbohydrates: 26g; Fiber: 16g; Sugar: 6g; Protein: 7g

ALMOND RAWMESAN CHEESE

This is a cheesy, rich, and savory addition to salads, soups, and pastas. Store in the freezer to prolong its freshness. Experiment with different nuts to mix up the flavor and texture.

Suggested Equipment: **Food processor**

1 cup almonds or Brazil nuts

1 tablespoon nutritional yeast

2 teaspoons garlic powder

½ teaspoon Himalayan pink salt

1. Pulse all of the ingredients in a food processor until the mixture reaches a texture like that of Parmesan cheese. Do not process too long or a paste will form.

2. Store cheese in a glass container in the refrigerator.

3. Sprinkle on soups, salads, and pastas.

Per serving (¼ cup): Calories: 214; Total fat: 18g; Sodium: 291mg; Carbohydrates: 9g; Fiber: 5g; Sugar: 2g; Protein: 9g

BUTTERNUT SQUASH VEGGIE-WRAPPED VEGGIES

PREP TIME: 25 minutes, plus dehydrating time | YIELD: 9 wraps

The batter is quick enough to prepare, it's the spreading into wraps that takes time. Be sure to make them consistent in thickness and thick enough to dry malleable rather than crispy. These wraps can be served savory or sweet. Try them with Dill Cashew Cream Cheese (page 88) and veggies, or Cashew Dream Cream (page 79) and fruit.

Suggested Equipment: **Dehydrator, High-speed blender**

1¼ cups flaxseed	1½ teaspoons Himalayan pink salt
½ cup sunflower seeds	1 cup water
2½ cups butternut squash, peeled and chopped	½ teaspoon cinnamon
	½ teaspoon curry powder
1 apple, cored and chopped	½ teaspoon turmeric
¼ cup plus 2 tablespoons psyllium husk powder	1 teaspoon cumin

1. Grind the flaxseed and sunflower seeds in a high-speed blender or grinder until finely ground. Transfer to a bowl.

2. Add the rest of the ingredients to the blender and blend until smooth. Add to the bowl with the ground seeds. Massage with your hands to mix well and to remove any lumps.

3. Spread evenly into circular wrap shapes on nonstick dehydrator sheets or parchment paper using a spatula, making sure not to leave any holes.

4. Dehydrate at 115°F for 4 hours, flip, remove nonstick sheet or parchment paper, and continue dehydrating for 1 more hour or until dry to the touch but still malleable. Be sure to respect the time as they will get too dry and won't fold like a wrap. If it is too dry in spots, sprinkle with a little bit of water. Store refrigerated in zip-top bags to keep soft.

5. To use the wraps, spread a layer of Dill Cashew Cream Cheese (page 88), Kale Caesar Salad dressing (page 99), or Zucchini Hummus (page 150), and a layer of Spicy Walnut Pâté (page 151) onto each wrap. Add fresh julienned vegetables of choice, such as spinach, cucumber, bell peppers, carrots, sprouts, or avocado. Roll up and enjoy.

VARIATION TIP: Try using these squash wraps to make fajitas! Use the Lentil Walnut Taco Salad filling (page 112) and all the taco fixings. If you don't have a dehydrator, use collard wraps.

Per serving: Calories: 197; Total fat: 13g; Sodium: 396mg; Carbohydrates: 23g; Fiber: 14g; Sugar: 3g; Protein: 6g

RAW VEGAN PIZZA

PREP TIME: 45 minutes , plus dehydrating time | YIELD: 1 large pizza or 4 individual pizzas

This is probably my favorite recipe, as pizza was once my go-to comfort food. I am still amazed at the amount and variety of comfort foods that can be made completely plant-based, raw, and vegan. My dehydrator can cook up anything that an oven can, leaving the nutrients and enzymes intact. Dress up the crust any way you like!

Suggested Equipment: **Blender, Dehydrator, Food processor**

For the marinade

2 tablespoons freshly squeezed lemon juice

2 tablespoons olive oil

½ teaspoon garlic powder

¼ teaspoon Himalayan pink salt

For the toppings

½ cup zucchini, diced

1 ripe tomato, diced

½ orange bell pepper, diced

½ cup spinach, chopped

½ cup pineapple, diced

½ cup cilantro or parsley, minced

½ cup olives, sliced

For the pizza crust

1 cup sprouted buckwheat groats (see pages 18–20)

½ cup flaxseed, soaked in ½ cup water

½ cup red bell pepper, chopped

¼ cup sun-dried tomato pieces, soaked 10 minutes in ⅓ cup water

1 tablespoon olive oil

1 teaspoon Italian herbs

½ teaspoon garlic powder

½ teaspoon Himalayan pink salt

½ cup Sun-Dried Tomato Sauce (page 137)

1. To make the marinade, combine all the ingredients in a bowl.

2. For the toppings, add all the ingredients to the marinade and let sit while you prepare the pizza crust.

3. Dehydrate the marinated veggies at 115°F for 1 hour.

4. For the pizza crust, place dry sprouted buckwheat in a food processor and process until finely ground. Let it stand in the food processor.

5. Into a blender, add soaked flaxseed, chopped bell pepper, tomatoes with their soaking water, and olive oil. Blend until smooth. Transfer to the food processor with the buckwheat and add herbs, garlic powder, and salt. Process to incorporate all ingredients into a dough.

6. If making small pizza crusts, divide the dough into four equal pieces and spread into 6-inch rounds on each corner of a nonstick dehydrator sheet. To make one 12-inch pizza crust, spread all the dough into a large round on the dehydrator sheet.

7. Dehydrate for 8 to 12 hours at 110°F, then flip, remove nonstick sheet, and continue dehydrating for 12 hours or until dry and firm.

8. Spread Sun-Dried Tomato Sauce on pizza crust(s) and top with warmed marinated veggies.

VARIATION TIP: Dress up the pizza any way you like. I like to use the leftover tomato sauce, pesto, ricotta, and Almond Rawmesan Cheese from the Raw Lasagna recipe (page 136). On top of that I add fresh elements such as alfalfa sprouts, sauerkraut, avocado, spinach, and tomato.

INGREDIENT TIP: When sprouting buckwheat, you'll need to soak the buckwheat groats for 30 minutes. After soaking, rinse very well in a colander as buckwheat creates a thick slimy starch. Leave the buckwheat in the colander on top of a plate or bowl so it has somewhere to drain. Spread the buckwheat around in the colander and leave in a cool dark place. Rinse two or three times a day to keep moist and encourage sprouting, for about two to three days until sprouts form. When tails form, sprouting has occurred. Let dry.

Per serving (1 individual pizza): Calories: 452; Total fat: 26g; Sodium: 589mg; Carbohydrates: 57g; Fiber: 15g; Sugar: 9g; Protein: 14g

Spicy Walnut Pâté
Cucumber Boats,
page 151

8 SCRUMPTIOUS SNACKS

MANGO SALSA

PREP TIME: 10 minutes | YIELD: 2 cups

Mango salsa is a refreshing sweet and spicy twist on regular salsa.
It works great as a dip for raw savory seed crackers or fresh vegetables
such as cucumber or bell peppers. Toss it on the Raw Mexi Chili
(page 95), Lentil Walnut Tacos (page 124), or any Mexican-themed dish.

1 cup cherry tomatoes, chopped

½ cup mango, diced

½ red bell pepper, finely chopped

¼ cup red onion, finely chopped

1 to 2 tablespoons jalapeño, finely
chopped

½ cup cilantro, chopped

1 tablespoon lime juice

1 tablespoon olive oil

Pinch Himalayan pink salt

Pinch paprika

Pinch chili powder

Combine all the ingredients in a bowl.

VARIATION TIP: Replace mango with pineapple.

Per serving (½ cup): Calories: 64; Total fat: 4g; Sodium: 9mg; Carbohydrates: 8g; Fiber: 2g;
Sugar: 5g; Protein: 1g

GUACAMOLE

PREP TIME: 5 minutes | **YIELD:** 2 cups

This is a nutritional powerhouse food that pairs perfectly with any Mexican-style dish. It also works great as a dip for flax crackers or fresh vegetables. Avocados are high in healthy fats and fiber, to keep you feeling full and your blood sugar levels balanced, which makes them a great addition to any meal.

Suggested Equipment: **Food processor or Blender (optional)**

3 ripe avocados

1 garlic clove, minced or pressed

2 tablespoons lime juice

Pinch Himalayan pink salt

Pinch cayenne pepper

½ teaspoon cumin

½ cup tomato, diced

1 tablespoon jalapeño pepper, finely chopped

¼ cup red onion, diced

¼ cup fresh cilantro, chopped

1. Mash the avocados with the minced garlic, lime juice, salt, cayenne, and cumin. Alternatively, you can prepare the guacamole in a food processor or blender and pulse until you get the desired texture.

2. Stir in tomato, jalapeño, and onion, and garnish with cilantro.

VARIATION TIP: Play around with the spiciness and the texture of the guacamole. I like to cut up my avocados and vegetables into small pieces so the guacamole is chunky. For a smoother, creamier texture, place all ingredients into the food processor and process until smooth.

Per serving (½ cup): Calories: 232; Total fat: 20g; Sodium: 15mg; Carbohydrates: 14g; Fiber: 9g; Sugar: 2g; Protein: 3g

ZUCCHINI HUMMUS

PREP TIME: 5 minutes | YIELD: 2 cups

I love hummus! It's easy to make, full of flavor, and gives life to boring cut veggies. Zucchini hummus is a great alternative to traditional hummus because you don't have to wait for the chickpeas to sprout in order to make it. Because zucchini is so hydrating, there is no need for olive oil in this recipe. Use as a dip for veggies or crackers or layer on a wrap or sandwich.

Suggested Equipment: **Food processor**

2 cups zucchini, peeled and diced

⅓ cup raw tahini

3 garlic cloves, minced

3 tablespoons lemon juice

½ teaspoon cumin

¼ teaspoon salt

1. Process all ingredients in a food processor until well combined. Scrape down sides as needed.

2. Store in an airtight glass container in the refrigerator.

3. Serve with flax crackers or fresh cut-up vegetables.

EQUIPMENT TIP: I like to use the food processor for making hummus. I find it the easiest. You can also use an immersion or high-speed blender.

VARIATION TIP: Substitute the zucchini for sprouted chickpeas or beets for a refreshing beet hummus.

Per serving (½ cup): Calories: 139; Total fat: 11g; Sodium: 465mg; Carbohydrates: 9g; Fiber: 3g; Sugar: 2g; Protein: 4g

SPICY WALNUT PÂTÉ CUCUMBER BOATS

PREP TIME: 10 minutes, plus soaking time | **YIELDS:** 2½ cups pâté

Pâtés are a high-protein staple in the raw food diet. Versatile, filling, and easy to make, pâtés make a perfect base for your wraps and rolls. This version stays fresh for a week in the refrigerator due to the lemon and salt.

Suggested Equipment: **Food processor**

1 cup walnuts, soaked

½ cup sunflower seeds, soaked 1 hour to overnight

1 cup carrots, chopped

½ cup zucchini, chopped

½ cup celery, chopped

¼ cup sweet onion, chopped

¼ cup fresh parsley, chopped

2 tablespoons lemon juice

1 tablespoon olive oil

1 tablespoon coconut aminos

1 tablespoon miso

1 tablespoon jalapeño, minced

1 garlic clove, minced

1 teaspoon cumin

Pinch cayenne pepper

1 large cucumber, cut lengthwise in half and then crosswise into 8 sections

1. Drain the walnuts and sunflower seeds well and pat dry to remove any excess water. You want the pâté to be thick, not watery.

2. In a food processor, pulse all ingredients except cucumber until well mixed. Continue to pulse, scraping down sides, until the desired texture is reached.

3. Cut cucumber into eight sections. Scoop out the seeds and pulp and stuff with pâté.

VARIATION TIP: To make pâté, you can use any nut or seed combination: sunflower seeds, pumpkin seeds, almonds, pecans, or cashews. Add herbs, vegetables, root vegetables, sauerkraut, salt and spice. Serve in cucumber boats, lettuce wraps, nori rolls, or as a dip.

INGREDIENT TIP: Use the scooped-out cucumber flesh in the pâté mixture.

Per serving (½ cup): Calories: 295; Total fat: 26g; Sodium: 211mg; Carbohydrates: 15g; Fiber: 5g; Sugar: 4g; Protein: 7g

CHEESY KALE CHIPS

PREP TIME: 25 minutes, plus dehydrating time | YIELD: 4 servings

Kale, like broccoli, is a member of the brassica family and has antioxidant, anti-inflammatory, and potent anticancer properties. Kale is low on the glycemic index and rich in minerals. If you have a garden, these chips are a great way to use up extra kale.

Suggested Equipment: **Dehydrator**

1 large bunch of kale, stemmed   **1 cup Cashew Cheese Sauce (page 130)**

1. Make sure kale is dry and tear the leaves into bite-size pieces.

2. In a bowl, mix the dry kale leaves with the cheese sauce, making sure to coat every leaf.

3. Arrange the cheesy kale leaves right on the dehydrator trays and dehydrate at 115°F for 8 hours or until dry and crispy.

VARIATION TIP: Kale chips can be tossed with a little olive oil and Himalayan pink salt for a salty chip instead of a cheesy chip.

Per serving: Calories: 199; Total fat: 13g; Sodium: 35mg; Carbohydrates: 18g; Fiber: 4g; Sugar: 3g; Protein: 8g

SALT AND VINEGAR ZUCCHINI CHIPS

Zucchini is a key player in the raw vegan diet as it adds substance, replaces noodles, and dehydrates into nice crispy chips. Zucchini chips are a high-fiber, low-glycemic, and healthy alternative to the traditional deep-fried potato chip.

Suggested Equipment: **Dehydrator, Mandoline (optional)**

2 tablespoons olive oil

2 tablespoons apple cider vinegar

1 teaspoon Himalayan pink salt

4 zucchini

1. Mix olive oil, vinegar, and salt in a large bowl.

2. Trim the ends of the zucchini and slice into rounds with a mandoline or knife, as thin and uniform as possible.

3. Add the zucchini slices to the bowl of oil and vinegar and mix well.

4. Lay the zucchini slices right on the dehydrator trays and dehydrate at 110°F for 4 to 6 hours, or until dry and crispy. Dehydrating time depends on how thick the slices are.

VARIATION TIP: Try making ketchup chips by mixing the sliced zucchini with the ketchup from the Jicama Fries and Ketchup recipe (page 155).

Per serving: Calories: 91; Total fat: 7g; Sodium: 601mg; Carbohydrates: 7g; Fiber: 2g; Sugar: 3g; Protein: 2g

SAVORY FLAX CRACKERS

PREP TIME: 20 minutes, plus dehydrating time | **YIELD**: ~ 50 crackers

Loaded with healthy fats and fiber, these crispy crackers will fill you up in no time. You won't be crushing the cracker box like you used to as your body will recognize the nutrients and let your satiety center know you've had enough. They go perfectly with dips, spreads, and pâté.

Suggested Equipment: **Dehydrator, Food processor**

1 cup vegetables (e.g., carrots, zucchini, celery, bell pepper, parsley, spinach, tomato, etc.), diced

½ cup onion, diced

1 cup flaxseed, soaked in 1 cup water for 10 minutes

¾ cup flaxseeds, ground

1 tablespoon apple cider vinegar

1 tablespoon soy sauce or coconut aminos

1 teaspoon garlic powder

1 teaspoon cumin

½ teaspoon Himalayan pink salt

Pinch paprika

Pinch cayenne pepper (optional)

½ cup pumpkin seeds, soaked

½ cup sunflower seeds, soaked

1. Process all ingredients except the pumpkin seeds and sunflower seeds in a food processor. Scrape down the sides as necessary.

2. Taste test and add more seasoning to your liking.

3. Transfer to a bowl and fold in sunflower and pumpkin seeds.

4. Spread a thin and uniform layer on nonstick dehydrator sheets or parchment paper. Score into cracker-sized squares and dehydrate at 118°F for 4 hours. Flip, remove sheets or parchment paper, and continue to dehydrate for 8 more hours or until dry.

VARIATION TIP: Use this basic cracker formula and add whatever nuts, seeds, vegetables, herbs, and spices you like. Get creative! You can also make a simple seed cracker with only seeds and seasoning.

Per cracker: Calories: 39; Total fat: 3g; Sodium: 48mg; Carbohydrates: 3g; Fiber: 2g; Sugar: <1g; Protein: 2g

JICAMA FRIES AND KETCHUP

PREP TIME: 20 minutes | YIELD: 4 servings

Fries and ketchup! Everybody's favorite. This yummy snack recipe doesn't need a dehydrator, as the sweet, nutty jicama has white crunchy flesh just like a freshly fried potato. Let the fries marinate for about an hour, covered, in the refrigerator, to enable the salt and oil to penetrate better.

Suggested Equipment: **High-speed blender**

For the fries

1 jicama, peeled

2 to 3 tablespoons olive oil (depending on size of jicama)

½ teaspoon Himalayan pink salt

For the ketchup

¼ cup sun-dried tomatoes, soaked for at least 30 minutes in warm water unless using oil-packed tomatoes

1 cup diced tomato

¼ cup red bell pepper, chopped

3 dates, soaked

1 tablespoon apple cider vinegar

1 garlic clove, minced

¼ teaspoon Himalayan pink salt

To make the fries

1. Peel and cut jicama into French fry shapes.

2. In a bowl, toss jicama fries with olive oil and salt.

To make the ketchup

Blend ketchup ingredients in a high-speed blender. Serve with fries.

PREP TIP: You can also dehydrate fries at 118°F for 2 hours or until as warm and dry as you like.

Per serving: Calories: 158; Total fat: 8g; Sodium: 516mg; Carbohydrates: 24g; Fiber: 10g; Sugar: 9g; Protein: 2g

CHOCOLATE ALMOND ENERGY BALLS

PREP TIME: 10 minutes, plus soaking time | YIELD: 15-20 balls

These energy balls are packed with fiber, protein, and healthy fat for a balanced and sustained source of energy. They are a perfect after-workout pick-me-up or afternoon snack. Dates have a higher ratio of glucose to fructose than any other sweetener. This allows for immediate energy usage as opposed to going through the liver first, as fructose has to.

Suggested Equipment: **Food processor**

¾ **cup dates, soaked in warm water for 10 minutes**

½ **cup almonds, soaked**

½ **cup unsweetened shredded coconut**

¼ **cup plus 1 tblespoon raw almond butter or peanut butter**

3 **tablespoons cocoa powder**

1 **tablespoon hemp seeds**

1 **tablespoon chia seeds**

1 **teaspoon vanilla extract**

Pinch Himalayan pink salt

½ **cup oats**

2 **tablespoons almond milk**

1. Drain dates well and add to food processor.

2. Add the rest of the ingredients to the food processor. Roll a heaping tablespoon into a ball. Repeat with the remaining mixture.

3. Store in refrigerator or freezer.

VARIATION TIP: Energy balls are a great opportunity to add more superfoods to your diet. Try adding maca, sprouted buckwheat, or superfood powders, such as dragon fruit or pomegranate.

Per serving: Calories: 124; Total fat: 8g; Sodium: 3mg; Carbohydrates: 12g; Fiber: 3g; Sugar: 6g; Protein: 3g

REAL FRUIT LEATHER

PREP TIME: 10 minutes, plus dehydrating time | YIELD: 1 roll, cut into 4-6 pieces

This is a perfect healthy snack for the kids that is really quick and easy to make. Real fruit, no added sugar, and full of fiber so they won't have a sugar crash. Enjoy with a layer of Cashew Dream Cream (page 79), or just enjoy them as-is.

Suggested Equipment: **Dehydrator, High-speed blender**

2 bananas

2 cups raspberries,
   fresh or frozen then thawed

1 tablespoon freshly squeezed
   lemon juice

1 tablespoon psyllium husk powder

¼ cup Cashew Dream Cream
   (page 79), optional

1. Blend bananas, raspberries, lemon juice, and psyllium powder in a high-speed blender.

2. Pour the mixture onto nonstick dehydrator sheets or parchment paper, and spread it ¹⁄₁₆ to ⅛ inch thick.

3. Dehydrate at 115°F for 4 to 6 hours or until the fruit roll is pliable. It should be a little shiny but not sticky. Peel off the nonstick sheet and continue to dehydrate for 1 hour longer.

4. Spread fruit roll with a layer of Cashew Dream Cream if desired, roll up, and slice into four servings.

VARIATION TIP: You can use ground flaxseed to replace the psyllium husk, use any type of berry you like with the bananas, or substitute 2 cups of mango instead of 2 bananas. You can also slice the fruit leather into strips and roll up.

Per serving (1 piece without cream): Calories: 61; Total fat: <1g; Sodium: 1mg; Carbohydrates: 15g; Fiber: 5g; Sugar: 7g; Protein: 1g

SPROUTED BUCKWHEAT GRANOLA BARS

PREP TIME: 30 minutes, plus soaking time | YIELD: 18 bars

These bars are convenient snacks for traveling. They are good to have on hand when you need a quick bite to eat. They will keep for a month or two when stored in an airtight container. Keep in mind, though, that the buckwheat needs to be sprouted for 24 hours first.

Suggested Equipment: **Dehydrator, Food processor, High-speed blender**

¾ cup almonds, soaked in warm water for at least 1 hour or overnight

¾ cup sprouted buckwheat

½ cup flaxseed, soaked

½ cup ground flaxseed

½ cup dates, soaked in ½ cup warm water for at least 1 hour or overnight and drained

1 banana

1 teaspoon cinnamon

Pinch Himalayan pink salt

¼ cup dried blueberries or raisins, soaked for at least 1 hour or overnight and drained

¼ cup goji berries, soaked for at least 1 hour or overnight and drained

¼ cup pumpkin seeds, soaked for at least 1 hour or overnight and drained

¼ cup coconut flakes

1. Process soaked almonds into almond meal. Leave in the food processor. Soak the flaxseed in ½ cup warm water for 30 minutes (no need to drain).

2. Add the buckwheat, soaked and ground flaxseed, soaked dates, banana, cinnamon, and salt to the almond meal. Do not overprocess. Transfer to a large mixing bowl.

3. Fold in blueberries, goji berries, pumpkin seeds, and coconut flakes.

4. Spread a thick layer onto nonstick dehydrator sheets and score into rectangles. Dehydrate at 118°F for 4 hours, flip, remove nonstick sheets, and continue to dehydrate for another 8 hours, or until dry.

VARIATION TIP: You can switch up the dried fruit, nuts, and seeds or add more superfoods such as cacao nibs, hemp seeds, and chia seeds.

Per serving (1 bar): Calories: 144; Total fat: 8g; Sodium: 9mg; Carbohydrates: 19g; Fiber: 5g; Sugar: 7g; Protein: 5g

RAW TRAIL MIX

PREP TIME: 5 minutes | **YIELD:** 2 cups

If you don't have a dehydrator to make granola bars, use the same ingredients to make trail mix. This trail mix makes a high-protein snack that is great on the road. Keep some in your glove compartment for those low-energy moments.

½ cup almonds

½ cup pecans

¼ cup dried blueberries or raisins

¼ cup goji berries

¼ cup pumpkin seeds

¼ cup coconut flakes

¼ cup cacao nibs

Combine all ingredients in a bowl and enjoy!

VARIATION TIP: You can switch up the dried fruit, nuts, and seeds to your personal preference.

Per serving (½ cup): Calories: 363; Total fat: 28g; Sodium: 30mg; Carbohydrates: 29g; Fiber: 9g; Sugar: 14g; Protein: 10g

Key Lime Cheesecake,
page 170

DELECTABLE DESSERTS

BANANA NICE CREAM

PREP TIME: 5 minutes | YIELD: 2 servings

Sometimes you just have to have ice cream! Banana Nice Cream is as dreamy and delicious as it gets. You would never guess that this easy-to-make sugar-free vegan ice cream is made with only three ingredients and is super healthy, too! Frozen bananas make the best creamy frozen dessert. Add your favorite fruit or berry and you've got Berry Nice Cream.

Suggested Equipment: **High-speed blender**

¼ cup dates, soaked

3 whole bananas, frozen

¼ cup coconut cream from a can of full-fat coconut milk

1 teaspoon vanilla extract

1. Drain dates well and pat dry. Add to blender.

2. Add the bananas, coconut cream, and vanilla to the high-speed blender and blend until smooth. Enjoy right away or store in the freezer.

VARIATION TIP: To make mint chocolate chip nice cream, add 1 tablespoon chopped fresh mint or a teaspoon of mint extract, 1 tablespoon cacao nibs, and blend.

Per serving: Calories: 288; Total fat: 7g; Sodium: 11mg; Carbohydrates: 58g; Fiber: 6g; Sugar: 36g; Protein: 3g

OATMEAL RAISIN COOKIES

PREP TIME: 10 minutes, plus 1 hour soaking time and 10 to 12 hours dehydrating time | **YIELD**: 2 dozen cookies

This recipe can be viewed as a cookie formula, which can be modified in many ways (see Tip). The hemp seed, coconut flakes, and pecans add healthy fats and protein, boosting nutritional value and balancing blood sugar.

Suggested Equipment: **Dehydrator, Food processor**

1½ cups gluten-free rolled oats

1 cup pecans

½ cup coconut flakes

¼ cup hemp seeds

¼ cup dates, soaked in water for 1 hour, strained, ½ cup liquid reserved

3 tablespoons maple syrup

2 teaspoons cinnamon

1 teaspoon vanilla extract

Pinch Himalayan pink salt

½ cup raisins, soaked in water for 1 hour

1. Add all ingredients to the food processor except for the raisins. Process until it begins to ball up, scraping down the sides as needed.

2. Fold in raisins.

3. Scoop 1 tablespoon of dough (a melon baller works very well) onto nonstick dehydrator sheets.

4. Flatten the balls into a cookie shape using your hands.

5. Dehydrate at 115°F for 10 to 12 hours.

6. Store in an airtight container in the refrigerator for maximum freshness. Cookies also freeze well.

EQUIPMENT TIP: This recipe can be a bit sticky, so I found a melon baller works great to get tablespoon-sized balls of cookie dough onto the nonstick dehydrator sheet. If you don't have one and need to opt for a measuring spoon, wetting the spoon before you scoop will help get the dough out easily. Wet your hands before pressing down on the sticky dough ball.

VARIATION TIP: Since this is a formula, you can change up the cookie flavor. For a banana chocolate chip cookie, add 1 banana, 1 tablespoon of cacao nibs, and 1 tablespoon of melted cacao butter; leave out the raisins, cinnamon, and nutmeg.

Per serving (1 cookie): Calories: 89; Total fat: 5g; Sodium: 1mg; Carbohydrates: 10g; Fiber: 2g; Sugar: 5g; Protein: 2g

RAW APPLE PIE

PREP TIME: 30 minutes, plus soaking time | **YIELD:** 4 to 6 servings

If you're in charge of bringing the dessert to family dinner, the Raw Apple Pie will be a sure hit. Place in the dehydrator to warm before serving and top with a scoop of Banana Nice Cream (page 162).

Suggested Equipment: **Food processor, High-speed blender**

For the crust

2 cups almonds, soaked 1 hour

1 cup dates, soaked

Pinch Himalayan pink salt

For the apple filling

4 apples, cored and chopped, divided

½ cup dates, soaked in water for 20 minutes

2 teaspoons soft coconut oil

1 tablespoon ground chia seeds

1 teaspoon cinnamon

2 tablespoons lemon juice

To make the crust

1. Drain the almonds well and process to almond meal. Add dates and salt, and continue to process.

2. Press the crust into the bottom of a cake pan or round casserole dish.

To make the filling and assemble the pie

1. Blend one-quarter of the chopped apples, dates, coconut oil, ground chia seeds, and cinnamon until smooth.

2. Process the remaining apples and lemon juice until chunky.

3. Add the blended apple mixture to the processed apples and briefly pulse until well mixed.

4. Pour the apple filling onto the crust and refrigerate; or to serve warm, dehydrate for 2 hours.

INGREDIENT TIP: Fresh or dried figs work as a substitute for dates.

Per serving: Calories: 706; Total fat: 39g; Sodium: 3mg; Carbohydrates: 86g; Fiber: 19g; Sugar: 60g; Protein: 18g

DATE TRUFFLES

Forgot to prepare something for the staff potluck? No worries! Dig through your pantry and grab a few ingredients, process, roll, and you're set!

Suggested Equipment: **Food processor**

For the truffles

1½ cups dates, softened (see Prep Tip)

3 tablespoons cacao powder

3 tablespoons unsweetened shredded coconut

Optional coatings

Cacao nibs

Cacao powder

Unsweetened coconut, shredded

Pistachios, crushed

Walnuts, crushed

Acai, goji, or pomegranate powder

1. Place the dates, cacao powder, and coconut in a food processor. Process until a paste forms.

2. Roll a heaping tablespoon of the mixture into a ball and repeat with the remaining truffle mixture.

3. Choose a coating, sprinkle it onto parchment paper, and roll the truffle in it to coat.

4. Store truffles in a glass container in the refrigerator.

VARIATION TIP: To take this festive treat to the next level, insert an almond or pecan half into the center of the truffle.

PREP TIP: Soften dates by soaking them in warm water for 20 minutes. Drain well and pat dry before processing, as you don't want too much liquid in the mixture.

Per serving: Calories: 155; Total fat: 2g; Sodium: 4mg; Carbohydrates: 36g; Fiber: 5g; Sugar: 28g; Protein: 2g

RAW CARROT CAKE

PREP TIME: 35 minutes | YIELD: 4 to 6 servings

The beauty of a raw dessert is that you can't really mess up. Baking, on the other hand, requires precise measurements, as it's all about the chemical reactions between the ingredients under heat. Raw desserts can be manipulated until you get the taste and texture you prefer.

Suggested Equipment: **Food processor, High-speed blender**

For the cake

4 carrots, peeled and coarsely chopped chunks

1½ cups oats

½ cup pecans

½ cup shredded coconut

2 tablespoons maple syrup

1 tablespoon coconut oil, softened

1 teaspoon cinnamon

¼ teaspoon ground ginger

¼ teaspoon nutmeg

½ cup raisins, soaked in water for 10 minutes

For the frosting

1 cup cashews, soaked

1 cup zucchini, peeled and chopped

2 tablespoons maple syrup

1 tablespoon coconut oil, softened

1 tablespoon lemon juice

1 teaspoon vanilla extract

To make the cake

1. Place all cake ingredients (except raisins) in the food processor. Process until well combined but still textured.

2. Transfer to a bowl and fold in the raisins.

To make the frosting

Place all frosting ingredients into a high-speed blender and blend until smooth and creamy.

1. Gather four small Mason jars or parfait glasses. In each one, spoon in a layer of cake, then frosting, and repeat, dividing the elements equally between the jars. Repeat with three other jars to make four servings.

2. Store in freezer to harden and set. Let soften for 30 minutes before serving.

EQUIPMENT TIP: Instead of layering the cake in jars, try a springform cake pan or a mini springform cupcake tin. Another option for assembling the cake is to line a loaf pan with parchment paper and layer the cake and frosting into the loaf pan. Put it in the freezer to set, and then pop out and store in a glass container.

Per serving: Calories: 684; Total fat: 40g; Sodium: 93mg; Carbohydrates: 78g; Fiber: 10g; Sugar: 31g; Protein: 13g

MINT CHOCOLATE CHIP SQUARES

PREP TIME: 35 minutes | **YIELD:** 8 squares

I don't know about you, but mint chocolate is my favorite flavor combination. These squares make an excellent anytime dessert. Just make sure you keep them frozen until an hour before serving as they will lose their shape if they get too warm. If you had to buy a whole bunch of mint for this recipe, try one of the delicious infused water recipes (page 63) to use up the rest of the herbs.

Suggested Equipment: **Food processor, High-speed blender**

For the crust

1 cup walnuts or pecans
  or a mixture of both

¾ cup dates

2 tablespoons cacao powder

2 tablespoons coconut flakes

Pinch Himalayan pink salt

For the filling

½ cup loosely packed spinach

¼ teaspoon coconut oil, plus 2
  teaspoons softened coconut oil

1½ cups cashews, soaked in warm water
  overnight and drained

2 tablespoons maple syrup

1 to 2 tablespoons chopped fresh mint,
  or 1 teaspoon pure peppermint extract

½ cup zucchini, peeled and chopped

1 tablespoon nut milk

½ teaspoon vanilla extract

2 tablespoons cacao nibs,
  for sprinkling

To make the crust

1. Process all crust ingredients in a food processor.

2. Line a loaf pan with parchment paper so the paper hangs over the sides, creating a handle.

3. Press the crust into the bottom of the loaf pan. Put it in the freezer to firm and set.

1. Massage spinach with coconut oil to soften.

2. In a high-speed blender, blend the spinach, coconut oil, cashews, maple syrup, mint, zucchini, nut milk, and vanilla.

3. Remove the crust from the freezer and add cashew filling on top. Sprinkle with cacao nibs and return to the freezer to harden, about 1 hour.

4. Once firm, use the loose parchment paper to pull the dessert out of the pan and onto a cutting board. Cut into squares and store in a glass container in the freezer.

INGREDIENT TIP: The spinach is used to give the cashew filling its green color. Alternatively, for a deeper green, try adding ½ teaspoon of spirulina, matcha, or chlorella.

VARIATION TIP: If you are trying to cut down on your sugar intake, replace the maple syrup with a few drops of monk fruit sweetener.

Per serving: Calories: 337; Total fat: 24g; Sodium: 8mg; Carbohydrates: 29g; Fiber: 4g; Sugar: 15g; Protein: 7g

KEY LIME CHEESECAKE

PREP TIME: 35 minutes | YIELD: 8 servings

A dessert chapter wouldn't be complete without a cheesecake! This luscious nondairy cheesecake is a perfect blend of sweet and tangy that will keep your taste buds looking for more. Play around with the key lime ingredients and taste test until it's to your liking. I personally like it tarter and less sweet, so I add lots of lime juice and less maple syrup.

Suggested Equipment: **Food processor, High-speed blender**

For the crust

1 cup pecans

¾ cup dates

Pinch Himalayan pink salt

Pinch cinnamon

¼ cup unsweetened coconut, shredded

For the filling

2 cups cashews, soaked

¼ to ½ cup key lime juice

2 to 3 tablespoons maple syrup

2 tablespoons coconut oil, softened

½ teaspoon vanilla extract

Zest of 1 lime

1 lime wedge, for garnish

Shredded coconut, for garnish

½ teaspoon spirulina chorella or matcha, for color

1. To prepare the crust, place all the crust ingredients in a food processor. Press into a parchment paper–lined loaf pan. Place in the freezer to harden.

2. Blend the cashews, ¼ cup lime juice, 2 tablespoons maple syrup, the coconut oil, and vanilla in a blender until smooth and creamy. Add more lime juice and maple syrup, to taste. Add spirulina chorella or matcha for color, if desired. Remove the crust from the freezer.

3. Pour the filling into the crust and spread evenly. Return to the freezer to harden.

4. Garnish with a fresh lime wedge or lime zest and a sprinkle of shredded coconut. Store in the freezer.

INGREDIENT TIP: If you can't find key limes in your area, regular limes work just fine.

Per serving: Calories: 409; Total fat: 32g; Sodium: 7mg; Carbohydrates: 30g; Fiber: 4g; Sugar: 16g; Protein: 7g

CHOCOLATE AVOCADO PUDDING

PREP TIME: 5 minutes | YIELD: 2 servings

This is probably one of the fastest and easiest dessert recipes to make; just a quick blend and you're done! It's a great after-dinner treat to satisfy that chocolate craving. I like to add a tablespoon of psyllium husk powder to increase my daily fiber intake.

Suggested Equipment: **High-speed blender**

2 ripe avocados

½ cup dates, soaked or 2 tablespoons maple syrup

3 tablespoons raw cacao or carob powder

1 tablespoon nut milk

Pinch Himalayan pink salt

Shredded coconut, for topping

Cacao nibs, for topping

1. Blend avocados, dates, cacao, nut milk, and salt in a high-speed blender until smooth and creamy.

2. Divide into two bowls and top with shredded coconut and cacao nibs.

VARIATION TIP: To make this recipe even faster to prepare, use maple syrup instead of dates.

Per serving: Calories: 454; Total fat: 28g; Sodium: 32mg; Carbohydrates: 54g; Fiber: 18g; Sugar: 29g; Protein: 6g

WALNUT FUDGE

PREP TIME: 10 minutes | YIELD: 6 to 8 squares

Here's a healthy spin on traditional fudge. The usual recipes are extremely high in processed sugar and saturated fat, but these home-made fudge squares are just as decadent but full of healthy omega-3 fats, fiber, and clean energy. No empty calories here! It's a sweet treat you can feel good about.

Suggested Equipment: **Food processor**

1 cup dates

1½ cups walnuts

2 tablespoons raw carob powder

½ teaspoon cinnamon

½ cup crushed walnuts, for topping

1. Process dates, walnuts, carob powder, and cinnamon in a food processor until they are well combined.

2. Line the interior of a glass dish with parchment paper, making sure the paper hangs over the edges of the pan. Transfer the date and walnut mixture to the dish and pack it evenly with wet hands to keep it from sticking. It should be about 1½ inches thick.

3. Sprinkle the walnuts on top.

4. Place in the freezer for 30 minutes to harden.

5. Once hardened, use the parchment paper edges to pop out the fudge and place on a cutting board.

6. Cut into squares and serve. Store in a glass container in the freezer.

VARIATION TIP: You may have noticed that this recipe is quite similar to the crust recipes used in other dessert recipes. Press the walnut fudge firmly into a pan and call it crust!

Per serving: Calories: 331; Total fat: 25g; Sodium: 2mg; Carbohydrates: 29g; Fiber: 5g; Sugar: 20g; Protein: 7g

MANGO RASPBERRY SORBET

PREP TIME: 10 minutes | **YIELD:** 4 servings

This mouthwatering frozen treat can be eaten anytime and enjoyed by all! It's a healthy treat that won't leave you feeling sluggish or dashing for the restroom like dairy does to some. The coconut cream gives it a smooth, creamy finish while preventing a blood sugar spike from all the fruit.

Suggested Equipment: **High-speed blender**

2 cups frozen mango

1 banana, frozen

1 cup frozen raspberries

¼ to ½ cup nut milk

¼ cup coconut cream from
  a can of full-fat coconut milk

1 teaspoon vanilla extract

Blend all ingredients in a high-speed blender. Start with ¼ cup nut milk and add more as needed to blend until a smooth and creamy consistency is reached.

VARIATION TIP: Use any frozen berry you like, such as organic black cherries. Yum!

Per serving: Calories: 122; Total fat: 4g; Sodium: 17mg; Carbohydrates: 21g; Fiber: 4g; Sugar: 15g; Protein: 1g

MEASUREMENT CONVERSIONS

Volume Equivalents (Liquid)

US STANDARD	US STANDARD (OUNCES)	METRIC (APPROXIMATE)
2 tablespoons	1 fl. oz.	30 mL
¼ cup	2 fl. oz.	60 mL
½ cup	4 fl. oz.	120 mL
1 cup	8 fl. oz.	240 mL
1½ cups	12 fl. oz.	355 mL
2 cups or 1 pint	16 fl. oz.	475 mL
4 cups or 1 quart	32 fl. oz.	1 L
1 gallon	128 fl. oz.	4 L

Oven Temperatures

FAHRENHEIT (F)	CELSIUS (C) (APPROXIMATE)
250°F	120°C
300°F	150°C
325°F	165°C
350°F	180°C
375°F	190°C
400°F	200°C
425°F	220°C
450°F	230°C

Volume Equivalents (Dry)

US STANDARD	METRIC (APPROXIMATE)
⅛ teaspoon	0.5 mL
¼ teaspoon	1 mL
½ teaspoon	2 mL
¾ teaspoon	4 mL
1 teaspoon	5 mL
1 tablespoon	15 mL
¼ cup	59 mL
⅓ cup	79 mL
½ cup	118 mL
⅔ cup	156 mL
¾ cup	177 mL
1 cup	235 mL
2 cups or 1 pint	475 mL
3 cups	700 mL
4 cups or 1 quart	1 L

Weight Equivalents

US STANDARD	METRIC (APPROXIMATE)
½ ounce	15 g
1 ounce	30 g
2 ounces	60 g
4 ounces	115 g
8 ounces	225 g
12 ounces	340 g
16 ounces or 1 pound	455 g

REFERENCES

Hu, Frank B. "Plant-based foods and prevention of cardiovascular disease: an overview." *The American Journal of Clinical Nutrition*. Volume 78, Issue 3: 544S-551S. Assessed December 1, 2019. https://doi.org/10.1093/ajcn/78.3.544S.

Mahan, L. Kathleen, and Sylvia Escott-Stump. *Krause's Food, Nutrition, & Diet Therapy*, 11th edition. Philadelphia: Saunders, 2003.

Tschirsky, Oscar. *"Oscar" of the Waldorf's Cook Book*. Mineola, NY: Dover Publications, 1973.

Tuso, Philip J., Ismail, Mohamed H., Ha, Benjamin P., Bartolotto, Carole. "Nutritional Update for Physicians: Plant-Based Diets." *The Permanente Journal*. Volume 17, Issue 2: 61-66. Assessed December 1, 2019. 10.7812/TPP/12-085.

World's Healthiest Foods. www.whfoods.org

RESOURCES

Books

Davis, Brenda, Vesanto Melina, and Rynn Berry. ***Becoming Raw: The Essential Guide to Raw Vegan Diets***. Summertown, TN: Book Publishing Company, 2010.

Pedre, Vincent. ***Happy Gut: The Cleansing Program to Help you Lose Weight, Gain Energy, and Eliminate Pain***. New York: William Morrow, 2017.

Pollan, Michael. ***The Omnivore's Dilemma: A Natural History of Four Meals***. New York: Penguin Books, 2006.

Brazier, Brendan. ***Thrive: The Vegan Nutrition Guide to Optimal Performance in Sports and Life***. Boston: Da Capo Lifelong Books, 2008.

Mind Body Green

A full approach to wellness that weaves in the mental, physical, spiritual, emotional, and environmental aspects of well-being:
www.mindbodygreen.com

Nutrition Schools

There are several key schools to explore, including:
https://pachavega.com/
www.wigmore.org
www.hippocratesinst.org

Ordering Raw Food

There are a few reliable sources for ordering raw food online:
www.realrawfood.com
www.omfoods.com
www.upayanaturals.com

RawGuru

With a mission to raise healthy eating awareness, this website offers resources to make healthy, organic food accessible to people everywhere. www.rawguru.com

The Environmental Working Group

This nonprofit is dedicated to protecting human health and the environment: https://www.ewg.org

The Take Home Nutritionist

Author Heather Bowen's website, offering in-home meal prep, cooking lessons, nutrition consulting, custom meal plans, and much more: www.thetakehomenutritionist.com

Young and Raw

A website dedicated to making real food fun: www.youngandraw.com

INDEX

ACKNOWLEDGMENTS

I would like to acknowledge my mom Barb Bowen, and our friend Ron Wilson, who ignited my spirit and inspired my passion for nutrition and raw food. I would also like to send out a special thanks to Danielle Arsenault, the founder of Pachavega Livings Foods Education. Although I was already pretty advanced in plant-based cuisine before I took her course, Danielle's spirit and passion only fueled mine even more. I'm grateful for the knowledge, inspiration, and opportunities that followed and some of the recipes in this cookbook are influenced by and adapted from hers.

ABOUT THE AUTHOR

Heather Bowen lives in Calgary, Alberta, and received her Bachelor of Science degree in Food, Nutrition, and Health from the University of British Columbia in Vancouver. Her desire to learn and her passion for nutrition and wellness did not stop there. She continued her studies in New York, where she received her Holistic Nutrition and Health Coach designation, and then in Costa Rica, where she was designated an Advanced Raw Food Chef.

Specializing in gut health, weight management, and plant-based cuisine, Heather practices a preventative and functional medicine approach to healing that focuses on addressing the root cause of the problem, and more importantly, preventing illness through nutrition. She believes that many lifestyle-related diseases can be prevented or reversed by choosing whole foods, practicing healthy habits, and fostering a positive mind-set.

Heather dedicates herself to helping others find optimal health by one-on-one consulting, nutrition education, and custom meal planning. She also offers private in-home cooking lessons where she works with her clients to teach them the value and skill of meal planning and prepping.

Heather prides herself on her ability to create plant-based versions of processed comfort foods that still taste delicious! In this cookbook, she has included many of her favorite raw vegan recipes. More of her tasty creations can be found on her Instagram, @thetakehomenutritionist, and you can also visit her website, TheTakeHomeNutritionist.com.

Printed in the USA
CPSIA information can be obtained
at www.ICGtesting.com
JSHW061910090524
61726JS00006B/18